Old Testament 30 Interactive Stories for Young Children

Steven James

Standard®
PUBLISHING
Bringing The Word to Life

Cincinnati, Ohio

D1298712

Dedication
To Barbi

Thanks & Acknowledgments
Thanks to Trinity, Ariel, and Eden, for all of your enthusiasm, creative ideas, spontaneity, and weirdness. This book wouldn't be what it is if it weren't for you.
Thanks also to Pam and Dawn for your helpful ideas and suggestions,
to Ruth for encouraging me to write for her again, to Pamela for her friendship and continual guidance, and, of course, to Liesl who has stuck with me through it all.

Published by Standard Publishing, Cincinnati, Ohio
www.standardpub.com

Copyright © 2006 by Steven James Huhn

Printed in the United States of America

Cover design: Liz Malwitz Design
Cover illustration: Paula Becker
Interior design: Liz Malwitz Design
Editorial team: Dawn Korth, Ruth Frederick

13 12 11 10 09 08 07   5 4 3 2 1

ISBN 978-0-7847-1939-8

Table of Contents

30 Old Testament Interactive Stories for Young Children

Chapter 1

The Creation of the World

BASED ON: Genesis 1, 2

BIG IDEA: God created the natural universe out of chaos and darkness.

BACKGROUND: The Bible opens with the account of creation. Our mighty and powerful God created the earth and the heavens and all the galaxies when he said, "Let there be."

Nobody knows exactly when God created the world, but believing that he did is a central teaching of the Christian faith.

Our views of the origin of the earth are not based on science, but on our faith in the Scriptures. As Hebrews 11:3 says, "By faith we understand that the universe was formed at God's command, so that what is seen was not made out of what was visible."

KEY VERSE: "In the beginning God created the heavens and the earth" (Genesis 1:1).

Sometimes when teachers tell the story of creation they get sidetracked trying to get the children to memorize what God created on each day. While that's certainly an important aspect of this story, the most important thing to emphasize is that God created our world and called it good. Spend more time emphasizing that, and less time trying to get the children to remember the exact order of God's creating.

Typically, a story is about a teachable character who faces a struggle and makes a discovery that changes his life. The key is that the character is transformed through the story as a result of facing the struggle. In this story, God doesn't struggle with anything, nor is he transformed or changed in any way. However, everything else is! In this story, the world is transformed from darkness to light, from chaos to order, from nothingness to abundant life. Remembering that will help you as you shape the way you tell the story.

This story is an easy one to act out because it has so many changes, sounds, and different living things (animals, birds, fish). Read through the following script a few times to get a feel for how it moves back and forth from acting out the story to inviting the children to join you in saying the refrain. The refrain serves as a way to help transition from one day to the next.

OK, kids, today's story is about a great big change. It happened in a time before there were eagles or tigers or puppies, before there were sunsets or stars or hippos, or even bellybuttons!

(DAY 1)
Long ago, God was all alone. He had no people to talk to, and it was very quiet. But then God said—do you know what God said? "Let there be light!" Let's say that together: "LET THERE BE LIGHT!" And when God said that, light went zooming all over the place!

Pretend that you are a little ray of light shooting out across the dark sky! I wonder if we have any fast rays of light in here . . . Oh, my! I wonder if there are any rays of light that like to move in slow motion . . .

And God saw all that light shooting around the sky and he said (say this in an exaggerated, rhythmic way), **"That's good! That's good! That's very, very good!" Can you say that with me just like that? "THAT'S GOOD! THAT'S GOOD! THAT'S VERY, VERY GOOD!"**

(DAY 2)

The next day God spoke again and separated the sky from the waters of the oceans and the rivers and the streams. Hmm . . . I wonder what we could do to pretend that we're a bunch of clouds? Can you float like a cloud? . . . Can you drift across the sky?

Let's be waves in the ocean rolling toward the shore . . . Can you be a waterfall plunging down a mountain? . . . Let's be a little brook bubbling and skipping over stones in our path . . . or a stream zig-zagging its way across the land. . . . Can you fall down like a rain drop? . . . Good. Float like a cloud again. . . . Fall down like the rain. . . Float! . . . Fall! . . . Float! . . . Fall! . . . Float! . . . Fall! . . . Wow!

And once again God said *(say this as before in an exaggerated, rhythmic way again. You'll do it that way each time)*, "That's good! That's good! That's very, very good!" Let's do it together! "THAT'S GOOD! THAT'S GOOD! THAT'S VERY, VERY GOOD!"[1]

(DAY 3)

On the third day, God made the flowers and the trees! Let's all pretend to be seeds. OK, scrunch up small and now, let's grow . . . grow . . . Grow . . . GROW! Wow! We have some really big trees in here! Is anybody poison ivy? Oh, no! Don't touch me!

And after making all those flowers and trees, God said again . . . *(encourage them by your expression and voice to join you)*. Ready? "THAT'S GOOD! THAT'S GOOD! THAT'S VERY, VERY GOOD!"

(DAY 4)

On the fourth day, it was time to make the stars and the planets and the moon and the sun! So God said, "Let there be!" and there was! God made the twinkling stars—wiggle your fingers to show me how twinkly you are . . . Good! And God made the bright blazing sun! Show me a bright, giant smile as if you were a giant sun. Blaze at someone next to you . . . Wow! And finally, God made the moon to float around the earth. Pretend I'm the earth and float around me . . . Very nice! I never knew I had so many moons!

God saw all the stars and planets and the sun and they were all very good. So God said again, "THAT'S GOOD! THAT'S GOOD! THAT'S VERY, VERY GOOD!"

(DAY 5)

On the fifth day, God made all the birds to fly in the sky and the fish to swim in the sea. So, let's have all the girls be birds. Fly birds, fly! . . . And boys, you can be sharks. Swim around a little . . . Chase a bird—no! Just kidding! The sharks did not chase the birds. *(When you say that, a bunch of boys will probably attack the girls! Be playful about this. Have fun with it.)* I said the sharks did NOT chase the birds!

Well, let's switch: boys, you be the birds . . . OK girls, you're all sharks! . . . Then all the birds and sharks went to sleep for the night . . .

And God said—ready?—"THAT'S GOOD! THAT'S GOOD! THAT'S VERY, VERY GOOD!"

(DAY 6)

On the sixth day, God made all the animals that walk on the land and crawl on the ground. What was one of the animals God made that day? *(Allow them to respond and then act like that animal together. You may wish to do this with several animals.)* Great!

And he also made people! God used the mud to form into a man. Pretend you're playing in a sandbox, or a mud pit, and shape your mud into a person. . . . Then God breathed his Spirit into the man. Breathe on your mud person . . . And *ta-da!* He's alive!

God loved all those animals and people, so God said again, "THAT'S GOOD! THAT'S GOOD! THAT'S VERY, VERY GOOD!"

(DAY 7)

On the seventh day, God didn't make anything at all. He was still. Freeze. . . . He took a break from all his creating to teach people they needed to take a break from their work too.

God is stronger than anything—do you think he was tired? *(Allow children to answer.)* God never gets tired! Flex your muscles and show me how strong God is!

But God rested on this day so that people would learn to rest too. So, let's all lie down . . . *(yawn)* . . . I'm getting sleepy . . . Let's go to—*(snore)* . . .

Great! God was finished creating the world and I think all the animals and birds and stars and everything were thinking, "THAT'S GOOD! THAT'S GOOD! THAT'S VERY, VERY GOOD!"

The end.

Consider how you might use props to make the story more interactive. Children will remain enthralled and curious about what object you're going to pull out next!

Here is a suggested script you could use if you wish to use props. Before class, gather the props and put them into a large bag, box, or crate in such a way that it's easy for you to remember the order in which to pull them out.

Long ago, God decided to create the world! So, he said, "Let there be . . . *(pull out the flashlight)* . . . light! And there was light . . . *(shine it around)* . . . so it wasn't just dark all the time any more. That was on the first day of his creating.

And God looked at what he'd made,
And he liked what he saw.
"Very good," said God, "very good" *(or, you could use the refrain from the previous story).*

On the second day, God said, "Let the clouds separate from the . . . *(pull out the squirt gun)* . . . waters!" *(Shoot some of the kids!)* And it happened just like that!

And God looked at what he'd made,
And he liked what he saw.
"Very good," said God, "very good."

On the third day, God said, "Let there be . . . *(pull out handfuls of rice or grass or leaves and throw them at the children!)* . . . plants and trees!"

And God looked at what he'd made,
And he liked what he saw.
"Very good," said God, "very good."

On the fourth day, God said, "Let there be . . . *(pull out a paper towel roll and use it as a telescope)* . . . stars and planets and stuff in space."

And God looked at what he'd made,
And he liked what he saw.
"Very good," said God, "very good."

On the fifth day, God said, "Let there be . . . *(pull out a stuffed shark)* . . . fish and birds!" *(Make the stuffed shark attack you.)* Ah!

And God looked at what he'd made,
And he liked what he saw.
"Very good," said God, "very good."

On the sixth day, God said, "Let there be . . . *(pull out a teddy bear)* . . . animals that *(as you describe these actions, make the bear do them)* crawl and climb and run and jump!" And God also made . . . *(pull out a Barbie doll and a boy doll, maybe a green army man)* . . . people! Both a man and a woman.

And God looked at what he'd made,
And he liked what he saw.
"Very good," said God, "very good."

Then on the seventh day, God didn't say anything . . . *(pull out a pillow)* . . . Instead God took a rest to show people that they should take a day off every week too! *(Lie down.)* . . . Good night! *(Snore until the kids "wake you.")*

Summary

Long,
Long ago,
Before time had begun,
There was nothing but God.
No moon and no sun.
No sky and no stars.
No earth and no sea.
No, nothing existed . . .
'Til he said, "LET THERE BE!"
And as God said the words, it all came about.
The world he'd dreamed of came whirling out!

"Let there be!
Let there be!
Let there be!"
And there was!
Hyenas to laugh and mosquitoes to buzz,
Eagles to soar in the newly-made sky,
Burrowing worms and wet octopi,
Gators to tromp on the swampy shores,
Stomping gorillas and tigery roars,

Light in the darkness!
Life on the land!
WHAMO! KA-BLAMO!
The world began![2]

Chapter 2

Adam and Eve Have to Leave God's Garden

BASED ON: Genesis 3

BIG IDEA: God gave Adam and Eve the freedom to obey him or to disobey him. They chose to eat from the Tree of Knowledge and God punished them, but he also gave them a promise in which they could place their hope (see Genesis 3:15).

BACKGROUND: In the beginning, nothing separated people from experiencing intimacy with God. God was very close to Adam and Eve and would walk with them in the cool of the day. However, they chose to sin by eating the forbidden fruit. When God confronted them, they discovered that not only would they have to leave God's special garden, but that nothing would ever be the same.

KEY VERSE: "When the woman saw that the fruit of the tree was good for food and pleasing to the eye, and also desirable for gaining wisdom, she took some and ate it. She also gave some to her husband, who was with her, and he ate it" (Genesis 3:6).

This familiar Bible story doesn't have a happy ending—Adam and Eve got kicked out of the garden, no longer to walk with God in the cool of the day, and had to learn to live with pain, thorns, and hard work until they died. Whew! All of those negative consequences might be overwhelming to young children, so when you tell this story you'll want to emphasize that despite their bad choices, God still loved them, took care of them (providing them with clothes), and made a promise that they could trust.

Also, you may not want to get into a big discussion about death. Rather than emphasizing that Adam and Eve would die if they ate the fruit, emphasize that their choice of disobeying God caused them to become separated from God.

Help the children to understand that even though we call it "The Garden of Eden," it was not like a garden we might have today in our backyards; rather it was much more like a wilderness or a jungle. Obviously, a jungle has lots of opportunities for sounds and sound effects, which is good news for you, the storyteller!

Here's a script for an imaginary journey through the garden (or jungle!) of Eden to the scene of Eve picking the forbidden fruit from the tree. Imaginary journeys are fun, creative ways to set up for or introduce a story. You can come up with your own imaginary journeys by finding stories that have interesting scenes with lots of things to see, smell, or hear (jungles, wilderness, seashores, nighttime).

As you read (or tell) this imaginary journey, be sure to pause long enough for the students to do the actions wherever the ellipses (. . .) appear.

> **What do you think it sounded like long ago when Adam and Eve lived in the Garden of Eden? . . . Remember, this was a wild garden, more like a jungle than anything else. What kinds of animals do you think were there? . . .**
>
> **Kids, let's pretend we're in the middle of that jungle long ago! We're walking through the jungle. Let me hear some jungle sounds!**

Is it hot in this jungle? . . . Whew! Are there mosquitoes? *(Slap at imaginary mosquito bites.)* What other animals are in this jungle? Make the sound of an animal you think is in this jungle . . . Wow! This sure is a noisy jungle!

OK, let's keep walking through the jungle . . . Walk, walk, walk. . . . Oh, no! I hear something—it's a tiger! . . . Run! Run through the jungle! Run! . . . Whew!

Uh-oh . . . I stepped in the mud . . . Yuck! Now we have to walk through the mud, but at least the tiger isn't chasing us. . . . I wonder what other animal might chase us . . . Oh no! There it is! Walk fast through the mud. . . Don't slip and fall down . . .

Whew! Wow! What an adventure! And look, there are trees in front of us! Push the branches of the tree to the side . . .

Oh, my! What's that over there? . . . I think I see a woman talking to—she's talking to a snake! What could they be talking about? Everybody sit down . . . Let's listen and find out what's happening . . . and why a woman would talk to a snake. . . .

After doing the imaginary journey, you could tell the story of Eve in the garden as a monologue, or you could act it out as a skit, or read the story from the Bible. Here's a monologue that you (or another teacher) could use. Practice the story a few times aloud before class so you don't have to read it when you perform it for the children. You'll need an apple for this story.

Hmm . . . God told me not to eat this fruit *(hold up the fruit)*, but it looks so yummy! I really want to have some!

God said if I take a bite out of it I'll die, but the snake told me God was lying! Hmm . . . Who should I listen to—God, or the snake?

What should I do? *(Look at the fruit.)* This fruit sure looks good . . . *(smell the fruit)* smells good too. . . . Hmm . . .

God lets us have all the other fruit here in the Garden of Eden. Why won't he let us have this fruit too? What's his problem? It's not fair that we can't eat this fruit too! I think God is being mean by not letting us eat this fruit!

(Look both ways as if you're checking to make sure no one is watching. Then, hold up the fruit.) What do you think I should do? *(Allow them to respond, then turn your back to the students and take a big bite of the fruit.)*

Hmm . . . it sure is yummy! I think I'll give some to Adam to eat too. Yeah, that's what I'll do. God won't mind. It's not really that big of a deal. *(Take another bite of the fruit and walk away. Then, if you're teaching class by yourself, set down the fruit, turn around and say, "Well, if I really were that woman—whose name was Eve—I'd be in big trouble, wouldn't I?" This way they'll know you're no longer acting like that character as you lead the discussion.)*

After the monologue, lead the children in a discussion of what they think of Eve's choice. Explain that after she gave some of the fruit to Adam they both felt bad and guilty. **"Have you ever felt like that after you got caught doing something naughty? All the bad things we do separate us from God, but God's love can draw us close again."**

Be sure to explain that even though Adam and Eve had to leave God's special garden, God still loved them and offered them the promise of a Savior. **"All of us sometimes do things we're not supposed to do. But that doesn't mean God stops loving us! And it doesn't mean Jesus won't forgive us. We can learn from this story of Adam and Eve—not only about how we should obey God, but also about God's promises of love and forgiveness in those times when we disobey him."**

Summary

With sinning came dying and suffering and pains,
Decay and destruction and sickness and stains;
Things rotting! Things stinking!
Things making a mess!
And Eve wearing leaves for her shirt and her dress!
      (And Adam wore pants made of plants I would guess!)

They had to move out and start living with hope.
They learned about sweat and they learned about soap!
      As they faced the results of the choices they chose,
Yet, God offered a promise and sewed them new clothes!

For he still loved this couple, so he promised to send,
A Savior who'd suffer, yet win in the end!
He'd crush all the evil that led them astray—
      Yes, Jesus would stomp on the Tempter one day![3]

Chapter 3

Noah and the Great Big Boat

BASED ON: Genesis 6–9

BIG IDEA: God kept his promise to rescue Noah and his family from the worldwide flood. God keeps his promises to us today, too.

BACKGROUND: After God created the world, the people soon turned away from him. The rebellion on the earth became so bad that God decided to destroy his new world with a huge flood. However, Noah and his family trusted and followed God, and in the end God rescued them.

God told Noah to build a great big boat called an "ark." Then, God sent him two of each of the different types of animals in the world so that he could rescue them too.

God kept his promise to keep Noah and his family safe. God also sent the rainbow as a symbol of his promise to never allow another worldwide flood.

KEY VERSE: "Whenever I bring clouds over the earth and the rainbow appears in the clouds, I will remember my covenant between me and you and all living creatures of every kind. Never again will the waters become a flood to destroy all life" (Genesis 9:14, 15).

This story is rather violent—nearly the entire population of the world is wiped out! People were drowning, dying everywhere. You may not want to get into all that with children of this age group!

Instead, emphasize that God kept Noah and his family safe on the big boat while the storm came and the flood covered the earth. Also, you'll want to draw attention to the rainbow and God's promise never to allow another worldwide flood.

When leading the following sound effects story, have a partner do the sound effects while you read or tell the story. You may wish to have the students join the sound effects person and do the sounds and actions with her, or you may wish to just perform the story in front of your children.

If you have a helper who's creative and dramatic, you may not even need to give her the script, just let her make up the sound effects and gestures whenever you pause after each line! (Hint: For some creative people, this is even more fun than following a script!)

The empty spaces that appear after certain lines are simply there to break up the story and make it easier for you to find your place. (Note that, in order to make the story sillier, the sound effects person sometimes gets the sounds mixed up!)

THE NOISY BOAT *(a sound effects version of "Noah and the Ark")*	
WHAT TO SAY:	**SUGGESTED SOUND EFFECTS:**
Long ago, the people were very mean . . .	Err!
And when God saw that, he was very sad . . .	*(Crying)* Waa! Waa!
Um, God did not cry like a little baby.	Oh.
Instead, God told Noah to build a big boat. So Noah carried the wood . . .	*(Grunt.)*
. . . Nailed the boards together . . .	Wham! Wham! Wham!
. . . Maybe he accidentally hit his thumb . . .	*(Shaking your finger)* Ow!
But finally, the boat was finished!	*(Smiling)* Ta-da!

Then the animals started to come. There were sheep . . .	Baa.
. . . and dogs . . .	Woof! Woof!
. . . and octopuses . . .	Squishy! Squishy! Squishy!
Wait a minute! The octopuses didn't get on the boat; they stayed in the water . . .	Oh. Swishy. Swishy. Swishy.
. . . Anyway, with all those animals, there was lots of howling . . .	*(Howl.)*
. . . and roaring . . .	*(Roar.)*
. . . and hissing . . .	*(Hiss.)*
. . . and mooing . . .	*(Squeak. Squeak.)*
I said mooing, not squeaking!	Oh. *(Moo. Moo.)*
. . . and squishing . . .	Squishy! Squishy!
Then, God slammed the boat's door shut.	Wham!
I hope no one's toes were in the way!	*(Hopping on one foot)* Ow!
And then the storm began! The wind was blowing . . .	Whoosh. Whoosh.
. . . the thunder was booming . . .	Boom. Boom.
. . . and the people who didn't get on the boat were yelling!	Ahh!
And mean!	Err!
And sad!	*(Crying)* Waa! Waa!
Then, the boat floated on the water	Whee!
and the animals were excited. There was even more howling . . .	*(Howl!)*
. . . and roaring!	*(Roar!)*
. . . and hissing!	*(Hiss!)*
. . . and mooing!	*(Squeak. Squeak.)*
I said mooing!	*(Hiss! Hiss!)*
Mooing!	Oh. *(Moo. Moo.)*
. . . and squishing . . .	Squishy! Squishy!
For a long time, the boat floated on the water,	Whee!
rocking back and forth.	*(Rocking back and forth)* Whoa, baby.
and God took care of them all.	*(Smiling)* Ahh!
Until one day, dry land appeared	Ta-da!
and all the animals left the ark howling . . .	*(Moo!)*
. . . and roaring . . .	*(Hiss!)*
. . . and hissing . . .	*(Roar!)*
. . . and mooing . . .	*(Howl!)*
. . . and squishing . . .	Squishy! Squishy!
Noah and his family and all those animals were safe.	Ah!
And God promised never to send a giant flood like that again.	Hooray!
The end.	*(Bow to the audience.)*

Another way to tell this story would be to encourage the children to act like the various animals. This will help them get their wiggles out and be a little silly, while also helping them to more easily remember the story.

Read the following example once or twice to make sure you're comfortable with the flow of the activity before leading it with the children.

What was one of the animals that God sent onto Noah's big boat? . . . *(Allow them to respond. Choose one of the animals that seems appropriate. For the purposes of this script, I'll insert some ideas. But rather than use these, use the ones your students suggest.)* . . . Right! Good! Giraffes! God sent giraffes. . . . Let's all pretend we're giraffes . . .

What was another one of the animals that God sent to Noah to be safe and dry on the big boat? Good! Snakes! Wow, let's all pretend to be a bunch of snakes . . . *(Do this for a number of animals. Don't beat the idea to death, but allow the kids to have fun with naming and then acting like different animals for a little while.)*

OK, let's all climb onto the big boat! . . . Choose what kind of animal you want to be and let's all get aboard! . . . *(Lead the children around the room to a special place that can serve as the ark.)* . . . Now, at night the animals would sleep . . . But during the day they were awake and made a lot of noise . . . Sometimes they got a little wild! . . . Sometimes Noah would bring them their food and the animals would eat their favorite food . . .

And after eating, maybe they yawned . . . and stretched . . . and went back to sleep again . . . or maybe they ran around the boat getting crazy and wild! . . .

This went on for a long time . . . but then it stopped . . . I think the animals got tired of being on the boat. Maybe they were bored . . . or maybe they were sad. Show me how sad they might have looked . . . or maybe, angry! . . .

But one day Noah sent a dove to see if there was any dry land nearby. OK, now whatever animal you were before, be a dove now. Let's fly around . . . Looking for dry land . . . Can anybody find some? . . . Where? . . . Is it over there? Let's all fly over there . . . Nope, not dry enough. Where else should we look? *(Look in various places; have fun with it.)*

The dove finally found a tree and stopped flying . . . OK everyone, stop flying. . . .

Soon, Noah's family and the animals all left the boat and they were all very HAPPY! Let me see your happy faces! They were even happier than that! . . . Even happier! . . .

Then, once the animals got off the boat, all the animals got REALLY WILD! . . . Oh, you are good at getting wild!

God had kept his promises to them. And he keeps his promises to us today too! The end.

Summary

Long ago all the people were angry and bad,
Doing things that were naughty and making God sad,
So he asked Mister Noah to build a big boat
And he taught him the best way to make it to float.
Drop and drip,
Drop and drip,
Drop and drip drop!
Thunder boom!
Thunder boom!
Thunder boom POP!

Then God sent the animals climbing aboard;
And some of them mooed,
      Some barked
             And some roared!
Then God himself shut the boat's giant door,
And more rain started falling than ever before!
Drop and drip,
Drop and drip,
Drop and drip drop!
Thunder boom!
Thunder boom!
Thunder boom POP!

And the boat Noah built floated up on the sea,
While the animals inside were as loud as can be.
They were stuck in the boat as the raindrops fell,
      (And I think Noah's family got sick of the smell!)
Drop and drip,
Drop and drip,
Drop and drip drop!
Thunder boom!
Thunder boom!
Thunder boom POP!

Many months passed before the flood was all done.
Then away went the clouds and out came the sun!
Noah's family was safe, and the animals were too.
      God had rescued them all like he promised to do!

Chapter 4

Sarah Has a Special Baby

BASED ON: Genesis 18:1-15, 21:1-7

BIG IDEA: God kept his promise to provide a child to Abraham and Sarah, even though she was well past the age of childbearing.

BACKGROUND: God had given Abraham a number of promises, including honor, land, descendants, and a future blessing. Abraham and his wife waited a long time to see God's promise of descendants come true.

Through his life Abraham followed God's leading and, according to Romans 4:20, 21, didn't waver through unbelief regarding God's promises.

In this story, some angelic visitors arrive at Abe's house to reassure him of God's promises. Sarah laughs at the thought of bearing a baby, since it seems too good to be true. But about a year later the baby arrives, and this time Sarah laughs for joy!

KEY VERSE: "Sarah said, 'God has brought me laughter, and everyone who hears about this will laugh with me'" (Genesis 21:6).

While the accounts of Abraham and Sarah span many chapters of the Bible (and many promises of God), the following activities focus on God's promise of a baby boy, and Sarah's transformation from thinking it was ridiculous that she would have a baby, to rejoicing in the baby God allowed her to have.

When teaching this lesson to the children, be sure to emphasize that Sarah was too old to have a baby, that she was older than their grandmothers!

In this story, two men tell of God's promise, but then at times they are referred to as angels and one of them is even called the Lord. To simplify, I have referred to them as men throughout the lesson.

In the Bible, when Sarah overheard the promise of a baby, she laughed and when she was confronted, she lied and said that she didn't laugh. You could use that as an example of how we sometimes lie when we're afraid, but I wouldn't emphasize it too much because it isn't central to the story. This is more the tale of Sarah's struggle to believe God's promise than about telling the truth. Focusing too much on the lie could distract children from understanding the main point of the story. Listed below is a simple refrain to say with the children.

> Sarah and Abraham wanted a baby.
> They wanted a baby,
> They wanted a baby.
> Sarah and Abraham wanted a baby.
> They wanted a baby boy.

> Shh . . . for a long time it was quiet as Abraham and Sarah waited for their baby. It was very quiet . . . but when a baby arrives is it quiet anymore? . . . That's right! What does a baby sound like? . . .
> Right! But even though they knew it would be noisy . . .

> Sarah and Abraham wanted a baby.
> They wanted a baby,
> They wanted a baby.

Sarah and Abraham wanted a baby.
They wanted a baby boy.

God had promised to send a baby to Abraham and Sarah. But they waited a long time! One day some men came and repeated God's promise to send them a baby. They could hardly believe it! Sarah laughed. She thought she was too old to have a baby. But even though she was old . . .

Sarah and Abraham wanted a baby.
They wanted a baby,
They wanted a baby.
Sarah and Abraham wanted a baby.
They wanted a baby boy.

Then one day the baby came! And do you think they were happy! . . . Yes, they were! And when Sarah saw that baby she laughed . . . and the baby cried . . . and Abraham smiled . . . and the baby cried . . . and Sarah laughed . . . and then they were all quiet . . .

Sarah and Abraham wanted a baby.
They wanted a baby,
They wanted a baby.
Sarah and Abraham wanted a baby.
They wanted a baby boy.

It was time for Abraham and Sarah to thank God for their baby boy! Sarah said, "Everyone who hears about this will share my joy!" Because . . .

Abraham and I, we wanted a baby.
We wanted a baby,
We wanted a baby.
Abraham and I, we wanted a baby.
[And] God gave us a baby boy.

On the next page is a monologue, a special way of retelling a story from the perspective of one of the characters in the story. This story is told from Sarah's perspective. If you wish, wear a shawl, a woman's hat, or a wig when you tell the story! When learning a monologue, follow these seven steps:

1. Read it aloud three times. Don't try to memorize it word for word, just think through the flow of the monologue from one idea to the next.

2. Explain the monologue to yourself in your own words. For example, "This monologue is about . . ."

3. Try to go all the way through the monologue to the end, regardless of whether or not you use the "right" words or remember every detail.

4. Review the script. Look at the sections you forgot; don't worry about specific words; you're trying to make sure you know the sweep of the monologue. For example, this one starts by introducing Sarah's love for children, tells about the problem of her being too old to have children; moves to God's promise of a baby, her surprise, and then her joy when the baby finally came.

5. Practice it again without the script. Stand up and walk around as you tell it to see what actions feel natural to use.

6. Take a break. Put the script aside, wait a few hours or a day, then pull it out and try it again.

7. Continue reviewing the monologue without the script until you're comfortable with it. Only refer to the script if you get stumped. Remember to go all the way through the script each time rather than starting over if you can't remember a specific word. Relax and have fun!

Oh, kids it's so good to see you today. I just love kids! The only problem was, I never thought I'd have any kids of my own. You see, my name is Sarah. And I'm married to a man named Abraham. I call him Abe for short.

And a long time ago God promised Abe—for short—that we would have a baby. I'd waited so long for a baby. I'd waited so long I was old enough to be a great, great grandma. I was 90 years old!

And when Abe—for short—told me that God was going to send us a baby, I couldn't even believe it. I just laughed and shook my head. "An old lady like me with a little bitty baby? That's the funniest joke I've heard all year!"

Now when I look back, I think I should have believed the promise, because nothing is impossible with God. But at the time, it seemed too incredible to believe.

Then God told Abe—for short—that I really would have a baby. In fact, I would have a baby boy by the very next year. Can you guess who was right about the baby, me or God? Right! I had a baby boy and then I had to laugh at myself for not believing God in the first place! I said, "God has given me laughter and a giggling baby boy! Everyone who hears about this will burst out laughing too! Who would have ever thought that an old lady like me could ever have a baby!"

So kids, that's what happened. And it just proves that when God makes a promise, you can be sure he's going to keep it! Just like he did for me and my husband Abraham, I mean, Abe—for short.

Summary

Sarah was a woman
Who was feeling very sad.
For she wanted to be a mommy;
And she wanted it really bad!
  (And her husband, Abraham,
  Really wanted to be a dad.)

But they didn't have any babies
And the wait seemed very long.
And then one day a couple of strangers
Happened to come along.

The men told them that Sarah
Would have a baby within a year.
But it only made her laugh and say,
"That'll never happen here!"

But within a year it all came true
And Sarah had her son!
She laughed and laughed for joy at last
At what the Lord had done.

Chapter 5

Joseph Goes to Egypt

BIG IDEA: Through the good times and through the bad times, God was working behind the scenes in Joseph's life to bring a blessing to the land.

BACKGROUND: The epic tale of Joseph sweeps through more than a dozen chapters of Genesis. God revealed the future to Joseph in special dreams—something that bothered his eleven brothers. One day they sold him into slavery after considering killing him. Yet God continued to bless Joseph despite the evil intentions of his siblings.

KEY VERSE: "His brothers pulled Joseph up out of the cistern and sold him for twenty shekels of silver to the Ishmaelites, who took him to Egypt" (Genesis 37:28).

Since the story of Joseph's life takes up such a large chunk of the Bible, it would be tough to cover the whole sweep of the story in one lesson. This chapter only contains summarized versions of a few of the adventures (or misadventures!) of Joseph's life. By the way, you'll want to make sure the children don't think this Joseph is the same man who was married to Jesus' mother.

For the following story, have the children join you by putting on imaginary "masks." Also, have the children cheer, growl, and wail with you as you come to the happy, mean, and sad parts of the story.

Joseph lived in a family with 11 brothers and they didn't like him at all. They were very mean (*put on a mean mask, "Err!"*). . . . **Now, Joseph's dad loved him very much, and that made Joseph happy** (*happy mask, "Yea!"*) . . . **but when the brothers saw that, they were even meaner to him than before!** (*put on a mean mask, "Err!"*) . . .

One day, Joseph's dad gave him a special colorful coat and that made Joseph happy! (*happy mask, "Yea!"*) . . . **But you know how it made his brothers feel!** (*put on a mean mask, "Err!"*) . . .

Now, Joseph had some dreams in which his brothers had to bow down to him. That made Joseph happy (*happy mask, "Yea!"*) . . . **But, you guessed it—it made his brothers really, really** (*put on a mean mask, "Err!"*). . .

One day, when they were alone with Joseph, they threw him in a deep hole in the ground. The hole was called a "well" but really it was a deep, deep pit. Being thrown in there made Joseph mad (*put on a mean mask, "Err!"*) . . . **But it made his brothers happy** (*happy mask, "Yea!"*). . . . **They planned on leaving him there forever! That made Joseph sad** (*put on a sad mask, "Waa!"*) . . .

But they pulled him out and then he was happy (*happy mask, "Yea!"*) . . . **Until he realized they were selling him as a slave! Then he was mad!** (*put on a mean mask, "Err!"*) . . . **and sad too!** (*put on a sad mask, "Waa!"*). . . .

The men took Joseph to Egypt and sometimes he was happy (*happy mask, "Yea!"*) . . . **and sometimes he missed his mommy and his daddy and then he was sad** (*put on a sad mask, "Waa!"*) . . . **and sometimes bad things happened to him and he was probably angry** (*put on a mean mask, "Err!"*) . . . **but through it all, God was with him and in the end, Joseph was able to forgive his brothers and see his daddy again. And when that happened, everyone was very, very happy . . .** (*happy mask, "Yea!"*)

After telling the story, invite the children to act it out with you! Say something like this:

> Deep in a well, poor Joseph fell,
> When his brothers pushed him in!
> What was he going to do? Let's pretend we're in a deep, dark hole in the ground . . .
> How are we going to get out? Can we climb? Let's try to climb out of the hole! . . .
> Hmm . . . that didn't work. Let's try to jump out . . . See how high you can jump! Can you jump out of the hole? . . .
> Hmm, that didn't work either . . . maybe we can fly out of the deep hole! Everybody flap your wings! . . . Really fast! . . . Flap! Flap! Flap! . . . Oh, phooey. We can't fly out either!
> How else can we try to get out of this deep dark hole? *(Act out whatever they suggest, even if it's a little strange like "skateboarding" or "riding a spaceship." Have fun with it!)*

> Deep in a well, poor Joseph fell,
> When his brothers pushed him in!
> Oh, look! Someone is lowering down a rope! Grab hold of it! . . .
> Oh this must be good news! Here we go! Climb the rope . . .
> Yea! We're out of the well. Everyone sit down . . . wipe the sweat off your forehead from trying so hard to get out of the hole . . . And now, I have to tell you, that wasn't the end, but only the beginning of Joseph's many adventures!

Explain that after they pulled him out of the well, his brothers sold him as a slave—that means he had to work really hard and never get paid, and his master could always make him do stuff he didn't want to do!

(For this part of the story, you'll need four different coats. Before class you should probably practice putting on and taking off the coats so you don't need to look at the script when you tell this story to the children.)

WHAT TO SAY:	SUGGESTED ACTION:
Once long ago there was boy named Joseph. One day, his dad gave him a special coat!	Put on the colorful coat.
Oh, it was so comfortable and beautiful.	Twirl around. Show it off!
But one day, his brothers stole it from him!	Take it off, throw it to the ground.
They smeared blood on it and told their dad that Joseph had been killed!	Hold it up disgustedly.
Then, they sold Joseph into slavery, and all he had to wear were rags.	Put on the raggy coat.
He worked hard in Egypt fixing things around the house.	Pretend to fix a broken table.
Then, his master put him charge of everything in the house!	Take off the raggy coat, put on the nice coat.
But one day, his master's wife grabbed his shirt—we'll use this coat today—and pulled it off him!	Take off the nice coat and throw it to the ground.
She told her husband that Joseph had been bad, and her husband threw Joseph in jail!	Put on the raggy coat again.
One day, the king heard about Joseph and invited him to come and help solve a problem. The king had a dream he didn't understand and no one could tell him what it meant.	Take off the raggy coat.

So Joseph got cleaned up and went before the king. God told Joseph what the dream meant and Joseph told the king.	Put on the expensive coat.
And from then on, Joseph was in put in charge of helping people throughout the land! He helped them save up food so they would have plenty to eat in the days when no rain came!	Pick up the discarded coats and hand them out to the kids.
What his brothers planned for bad, God used for good!	Two thumbs up.
The end!	Bow to the audience.

Summary

Joseph's brothers did not like him
> One little bit.
So they put him at the bottom of a
> Deep, dark pit.
Then they pulled him out and sold him as a
> Slave far away.
To some men who were headin' off to Egypt that day.

When Joseph got to Egypt he was
> Put in jail.
It was dark. It was lonely 'cause he
> Didn't get mail.
And he sat in the dungeon for a
> Long, long, time.
Even though Joseph hadn't done a single crime.

Then the king had a dream that he
> Didn't understand.
And he brought Joseph up just to lend
> Him a hand.
[And] God explained to Joseph what the
> King's dream meant.
[And] Joseph told the king about the dream God sent.

Then the king was very happy that he brought
> Joseph in.
And he put him in charge of the
> Food collection.
Yes, God was with Joseph through
> Everything.
From the pit to the dungeon to the palace of the king.

Chapter 6

Baby Moses Floats Down the River

BASED ON: Exodus 1–2:10

BIG IDEA: God protected baby Moses when his mother placed him in the river.

BACKGROUND: After Joseph and his family settled in Egypt, their descendants had children and grandchildren who grew numerous and prosperous in the land. One day, a king who hadn't heard of Joseph became the ruler of Egypt. He was afraid of the Israelites, and oppressed them. Yet they continued to prosper. Finally, he ordered that all the Israelite boys be killed at birth. God used the situation to bring a great deliverer to his people.

Moses' mother, Jochebed, placed him in a basket and put him in the river where he floated to the princess's bathing area where she then found him and adopted him. Moses grew into a mighty leader.

KEY VERSE: "The woman took the baby and nursed him. When the child grew older, she took him to Pharaoh's daughter and he became her son. She named him Moses, saying, 'I drew him out of the water'" (Exodus 2:9, 10).

In this story, you'll want to avoid talking about all the slaughtered babies in Egypt. Rather, emphasize that when Moses was a baby, he was in danger and some soldiers wanted to hurt him, but that his mother did all she could to hide and protect him.

Many of your students have heard of Moses and know about his adventures with the burning bush, the ten plagues, and the Ten Commandments. When some young children think of babies in the Bible, they usually think of Jesus. So, to help them make the differentiation, be sure to tell them that baby Moses lived a long time before baby Jesus was born.

For the following version of the story, ideally you'll have a "baby" and a "basket" for each of the children. You could use toys, food, or dolls.

Also, lay a blue blanket on the floor. This blanket will serve as the "river" in the story.

> **Long ago a king in Egypt told the mommies to get rid of their babies—was that a very kind thing to do? No, it wasn't! One mommy named Jochebed had a baby boy named Moses. She hid him for a while. Where would you hide your baby? Behind your back? . . . Everybody hide your baby! . . . Be gentle! Don't hurt your little babies! . . .**
>
> **But when her baby got too big to hide, she had to do something else because he started to cry! Shh, little baby . . . What do you think he sounded like when he was crying? . . . If the soldiers heard the baby crying, they'd hurt him!**
>
> **Show me how scared his mommy looked! . . . Now, she knew the princess took baths in the river. Set down your babies for a moment and pretend you're in a bathtub . . . Scrub your underarms . . . Wash your nose . . . Clean your hair . . . Scrub your bellybutton! . . .**
>
> **Jochebed knew the princess was bathing in the river. So she put her baby in a floating basket . . . put your babies in their baskets. . . . She set him in the river . . . *(coach the children to put their "babies" on the blue blanket)* and he floated downstream . . . *(pull the blanket***

through the room. Be careful not to let any of the babies fall off!) **until he came to the princess!**

OK, now you get to pretend to be the princess!—boys, I guess you get to be a prince. She picked up the baby . . . go get your babies . . . hugged him . . . kissed him . . . changed his stinky diaper—no, she didn't do that; instead his mommy came to do that! And then when Moses got older he got to live in the palace with the princess!

The end!

When leading the following sound effects story, remember to practice it a couple of times before class to learn the rhythm of the sound effects. Remind the children that you'll be saying each refrain one time through, and then they'll join along in saying it two more times. **"Remember, we'll only do each sound three times so we can all hear the rest of the story!"**

Feel free to use appropriate voice inflection as you tell the story. For example, during scary parts you can make your voice sound scared, or during happy parts sound happy and relieved.

THE BOY IN THE ITTY, BITTY BOAT
(a sound effects version of "Moses in the River")

STORY:	REFRAINS:
When the king told the mommies to get rid of their babies, one mommy hid her baby.	Hide. Hide. Hide-y hide. Hide. Hide. Hide-y hide. Hide. Hide. Hide-y hide.
Until he got too big to hide.	Waa! Waa! Waa-y waa! Waa! Waa! Waa-y waa! Waa! Waa! Waa-y waa!
Then, she made a little boat for him. And she put the boat into the river.	Float. Float. Floaty float. Float. Float. Floaty float. Float. Float. Floaty float.
Baby Moses floated down the river past the crocodiles!	Chomp! Chomp! Chompy chomp! Chomp! Chomp! Chompy chomp! Chomp! Chomp! Chompy chomp!
Maybe he even went down a little waterfall!	Splash. Splash. Splashy splash! Splash. Splash. Splashy splash! Splash. Splash. Splashy splash!
He floated up to the princess who was taking a bath.	Scrub. Scrub. Scrubby scrub. Scrub. Scrub. Scrubby scrub. Scrub. Scrub. Scrubby scrub.
She thought he was such a cute little baby.	Koo. Koo. Kootchie koo. Koo. Koo. Kootchie koo. Koo. Koo. Kootchie koo.
She paid his mommy to take care of him—to feed him.	Yum. Yum. Yummy yum. Yum. Yum. Yummy yum. Yum. Yum. Yummy yum.
Talk baby talk to him.	Gaa. Gaa. Gaa-y gaa. Gaa. Gaa. Gaa-y gaa. Gaa. Gaa. Gaa-y gaa.
And change his stinky diapers!	Yuck. Yuck. Yucky yuck. Yuck. Yuck. Yucky yuck. Yuck. Yuck. Yucky yuck.
Moses had a new home!	Home. Home. Home sweet home. Home. Home. Home sweet home. Home. Home. Home sweet home.

He was safe from the soldiers!	Hip. Hip. Hip hooray! Hip. Hip. Hip hooray! Hip. Hip. Hip hooray!
The end!	

You could also tell this story as a call and response story, in which you teach the children to say or do something when you say special words. For example:

Mean king—"Err!"

Baby Moses—"Waa!"

Kind princess—*(Smiling)* "Aw!"

Finally, just for fun, you may wish to sing this silly song about Moses floating down the river.

MOSES IN THE RIVER
(Sing to the tune of "Row, Row, Row Your Boat.")

Row, row, row your boat gently down the Nile,
Try not to get swallowed by a hungry crocodile.

Row, row, row your basket gently in the path
Of the princess and her ducky floating in the bath.

Summary

The king was very mean
And he had a nasty plan,
To get rid of baby boys that
Were born in the land.
But one mommy said,
"I'm saving my kid!"
So she hid him
    And helped him
        And here's what she did:
She went to the river
And made a small boat
And she put the boy in it,
And sent it to float,
To the place where the princess
Washed off all her dirt,
And he arrived safe,
    And sound,
        And unhurt.
So the princess adopted that baby boy,
And she named him Moses
And he brought her great joy.
And Moses grew strong
With the Lord as his guide.
As God helped him
    And loved him
        And stayed by his side.

Chapter 7

Moses Sees a Burning Bush

BASED ON: Exodus 3, 4

BIG IDEA: God calls Moses to lead the Israelites out of Egypt.

BACKGROUND: After Moses killed an Egyptian guard who was mistreating a fellow Hebrew, Moses fled Egypt and became a shepherd in a nearby country. For 40 years he watched over sheep until one day he saw a bush that was on fire but didn't burn up.

           When he went to investigate the burning bush, God spoke to him and asked him to lead the Israelites to the Promised Land. Although Moses wasn't quick to say "yes" to God, God still decided to use Moses to lead his people. Eventually Moses became one of the greatest leaders and prophets the world has ever known.

KEY VERSE: "The cry of the Israelites has reached me, and I have seen the way the Egyptians are oppressing them. So now, go. I am sending you to Pharaoh to bring my people the Israelites out of Egypt" (Exodus 3:9, 10).

You do not need to emphasize that Moses fled Egypt because he killed a man. If you're concerned about this aspect of the story, you could say that after Moses grew up in Egypt, he left his country to start a new life somewhere else (after all, according to Hebrews 11:27, Moses didn't leave Egypt out of fear of the king's anger). Eventually, Moses became a shepherd.

Help your children understand what shepherds do by explaining that they camp in the mountains and protect their sheep from wolves. They have to be brave and strong.

Children might ask why Moses had to take off his shoes in this story. You can simply tell them that in those days it was a way of showing respect to someone important, and that there's no one more important than God.

Before starting this story, read through this script to become familiar with how it flows. Decide whether or not you want to include the introduction.

INTRODUCTION

How many of you have ever been to a campfire? . . . *(raise your hand to signal to them that they are to respond by raising their hands rather than by replying verbally)* **Ever roasted marshmallows? . . .** *(raise your hand again).* **Ever gotten gooey marshmallowy stuff in your hair? . . . Yeah, that's no fun . . . Well, then you know that when wood is on fire, it burns away, right? . . . So once you've burned wood do you have more wood or less wood than when you started? . . . Right! Less wood. But today's story is about a special fire long ago that didn't burn up the wood! There was just as much left over at the end as there was at the start! And this story is even more special because, while the bush burned, someone spoke from inside the fire.**

STORY

Once, long ago, Moses was walking along a trail in the mountains. Everyone, pretend you're walking along a mountain trail . . . Is it steep? . . . Is it hard to walk on? . . . Don't slip and fall down the side of the mountain! . . . *(If kids fall down say something like, "Oh no! Bobby fell down the mountain! Someone help him up!")*

Nearby were his sheep. What did they sound like? . . . Good!

Well, suddenly, Moses saw a bush burning, but the wood wasn't getting burned up! It's

right over there . . . *(point to the bush)*. He was surprised! Show me how surprised he was . . . Good!

Then, a loud voice came from inside the bush. Who do you think it was? Was it . . . *(List people your students might be familiar with, such as the president, Elmo, or Dora. Allow them to respond.)*

No! It was God! And God said, "Take off your sandals! Let me see your feet! This land is holy and special to me!"

Well, go ahead. Everyone take off your shoes. . . . I hope no one has stinky feet! . . . Do you think Moses had stinky feet? . . . The Bible doesn't tell us if he did or not, but it does say that God asked Moses to lead his people. At first, Moses didn't want to be a part of God's plan. He shook his head "no."

Pretend to be Moses. I'll pretend to be God, OK? Now, God told Moses his name was "Yahweh." So each time I ask you a question, shout, "NO WAY, YAHWEH!"

"Go and help my people!" *(Allow them to respond: "No way, Yahweh!")*
"Be the leader in the land!" *(Allow them to respond: "No way, Yahweh!")*
"Tell them what I say you should! *("No way, Yahweh!")*
"Go and take command!" *("No way, Yahweh!")*

(Getting a little angrier this time . . .)
"I said, go and help my people!" *("No way, Yahweh!")*
"Be the leader in the land!" *("No way, Yahweh!")*
"Tell them what I say you should!" *("No way, Yahweh!")*
"Go and take command!" *("No way, Yahweh!")*

(Do it one last time, even more sternly.)
"Moses, you're not listening very well. I said GO AND HELP MY PEOPLE!" *("No way, Yahweh!")*
"BE THE LEADER IN THE LAND!" *("No way, Yahweh!")*
"TELL THEM WHAT I SAY YOU SHOULD!" *("No way, Yahweh!")*
"GO AND TAKE COMMAND!" *("No way, Yahweh!")*

Now boys and girls, do you think Moses was making God very happy by telling him "No!"? . . . *(Note: some will probably say, "No way, Yahweh!")* That's right, God finally became angry and told Moses that HE was in charge and that he wanted Moses to go. So finally Moses said, "OK, Yahweh!" Let's say that together: "OK, YAHWEH!"

You could stop here to discuss the previous story, or you could transition right into acting out the calling of Moses.

Now, I didn't tell you this earlier, but God had allowed Moses to do some miracles. He did this so that Moses could prove he was speaking for God when he went before the king. A miracle is something special that can only be done by the power of God.

While Moses had been talking to God by the burning bush, God had told him, "Moses! Throw down your shepherd's staff!" And Moses threw his walking stick onto the ground. When he did, it turned into a snake! Then, God told him to pick it up again. And when he did, it turned back into a walking stick again. Let's act that out!

Stiff as a staff in Moses' hand. *(stand straight and stiff and tall)*
Then thrown to the dirt way down in the sand. *(flop to the ground)*
And hisssssss . . . slither like a snake. *(slither and hiss)*
And hisssssss . . . slither like a snake. *(slither and hiss)*
Slither like a snake in the sand! *(slither and hiss)*

Then once again.

> **Stiff as a staff in Moses' hand.** *(stand straight and stiff and tall)*
> **Then thrown to the dirt way down in the sand.** *(flop to the ground)*
> **And hisssssss . . . . slither like a snake.** *(slither and hiss)*
> **And hisssssss . . . . slither like a snake.** *(slither and hiss)*
> **Slither like a snake in the sand!** *(slither and hiss)*

Repeat several times. Each time through, get faster and faster! Have fun with it! Then say, **"Who changed that staff into a snake? That's right! God did. God wanted everyone to know that he was in control!"**

End by chanting this summary of the story together.

> **Once there was a man who was lookin' at his sheep,** *(Look around)*
> **Lookin' at his sheep.** *(Look around)*
> **Lookin' at his sheep.** *(Look around)*
> **Once there was a man who was lookin' at his sheep,** *(Look around)*
> **When he saw a burnin' bush!** *(Warm your hands by a campfire)*

> **Once there was a man and he knelt in the sand,** *(Kneel)*
> **Knelt in the sand.**
> **Knelt in the sand.**
> **Once there was a man and he knelt in the sand,**
> **And he took his sandals off!** *(Pantomime taking off shoes)*

> **Once there was a voice that came from a bush,** *(Point to the bush)*
> **Came from a bush.**
> **Came from a bush.**
> **Once there was a voice that came from a bush,**
> **And the voice came from the Lord!** *(Cup hand by ear as if listening intently)*

> **Once God's people had no one to lead,** *(Shake your head)*
> **No one to lead.**
> **No one to lead.**
> **Once God's people had no one to lead,**
> **So Moses was sent by God!** *(Nod head)*

Summary

(If you have older students, you could chant these verses as a round!)

Moses on the mountain.
Moses watching sheep.
Moses by the hills and the valleys deep.

Talkin' to a bush,
Thinkin' it was odd,
'Til he found out that the voice was God's.

Goin' down to Egypt
Meetin' with the king.
Here come the plagues—Zing! Zang! Zing!

Chapter 8

God Sends Ten Plagues

BASED ON: Exodus 5–12

BIG IDEA: When the pharaoh of Egypt refused to let God's people go, God sent a series of disasters on the land, bringing glory to himself and freedom to his people. God delivered his people from slavery.

BACKGROUND: Many years earlier Joseph had become the second most powerful man in Egypt. The pharaoh had encouraged him to invite his family to live with him. The Hebrews moved to Egypt and their numbers grew.

In time, a new pharaoh came to power who didn't know about Joseph. He enslaved the Israelites and for hundreds of years they were in bondage. But God heard their cries and called Moses to lead the people to freedom. However, the new pharaoh refused to let God's people go, and as a result, God sent a series of devastating disasters on the land.

KEY VERSE: "Moses and Aaron went to Pharaoh and said, 'This is what the LORD, the God of Israel, says: "Let my people go, so that they may hold a festival to me in the desert."'

Pharaoh said, 'Who is the LORD, that I should obey him and let Israel go? I do not know the LORD and I will not let Israel go'" (Exodus 5:1, 2).

Even though this story has some violence in it, it's a good story to act out because of the dramatic plagues! Just be sensitive to the developmental level of the students.

You'll probably want to avoid talking about the suffering of the people, and, while it's important to talk about the Passover, don't dwell on the fact that the Egyptians lost loved ones, but rather that God's anger passed over the Israelites and they weren't hurt.

As you retell this story, do the actions with the children. Don't just read the ideas from the book and tell them to do the actions. They'll follow your lead, so if you stand still, they'll probably stand still. But if you act it out, they'll be even more enthusiastic about joining in!

(You won't read the section headings aloud. They're simply there to help you keep your place.)

Moses told the leader of the land, "Let God's people go!" But the king said, "No!"

For this story, you kids get to be the bad king! I'll act like Moses and I'll say, "Will you let them go?" And then you say, "No! No! No!" Say it whiny and loud, OK? Let's practice: "Will you let them go?" . . . *(put your hand up to your ear to indicate to them to yell).* **"NO! NO! NO!"**

Wow! Good job. Remember to say it only three times. OK, I think we're ready to start the story. Besides being the bad king, I'll also give you special things to do during the story.

(PLAGUE #1: WATER INTO BLOOD)

Long ago, God sent Moses to ask the king to let God's people leave the land. Moses said, "Will you let them go?" . . . "NO! NO! NO!"

So then God turned the water of the river into blood. Yuck! Let's pretend we're floating in the water . . . swim around a little bit . . . swimming . . . backstroke . . . OK, good.

And Moses asked again, "Will you let them go?" . . . "NO! NO! NO!"

(PLAGUE #2: FROGS)

So this time, God sent lots and lots of frogs! Let's all hop like a frog. And hop . . . and hop . . . and hop, hop, hop . . . And hippity-hop, hippity-hop, hop, hop, hop!

And Moses said, "Will you let them go?" . . . "NO! NO! NO!"

(PLAGUE #3: GNATS)

So this time, God sent little buggy creatures called gnats . . . They climbed on the people and got in their ears and eyes and noses and bellybuttons! Show me a little buggy, gnatty face . . . Oh, you kids make a good group of bugs . . .

Moses said, "Will you let them go?" . . . "NO! NO! NO!"

(PLAGUE #4: FLIES)

This time, flies came! Everybody, pretend you're a fly! And buzz around and buzz . . . buzz . . . buzz . . . fly faster . . . and slower . . . and faster . . . and slower . . . fast . . . slow . . .

Moses said, "Will you let them go?" . . . "NO! NO! NO!"

(PLAGUE #5: DYING LIVESTOCK)

Next, the cows got sick! Pretend you're a sick cow! . . . What sound do you make? . . . Oh, listen to all those sick cows, it makes me so sad!

Moses said, "Will you let them go?" . . . "NO! NO! NO!"

(PLAGUE #6: SORES ON THE PEOPLE)

So this time the *people* got the big owies and boo-boos! Oh no! Where is your owie? On your arm . . . Your leg? . . . On your bellybutton! . . . Does it hurt? . . . What sound do you make when you have a big owie like that? . . . Oh, my goodness! Listen to that!

Moses said, "Will you let them go?" . . . "NO! NO! NO!"

(PLAGUE #7: HAIL)

Suddenly a big storm came! Watch out! It's starting to rain . . . Now it's not just raining, it's hailing! . . . Oh, no, is the hail bonking you on the head? . . . Ouch! . . .

"Will you let them go?" . . . "NO! NO! NO!"

(PLAGUE #8: LOCUSTS)

Next came the big, hungry grasshoppers! They jumped around like this! *(demonstrate)* . . . Let's see you jump around like a bunch of grasshoppers! . . . Are you hungry grasshoppers? Are you eating everything in sight? Oh, no! Show me how hungry you are . . .

"Will you let them go?" . . . "NO! NO! NO!"

(PLAGUE #9: DARKNESS)

Then, God made it very dark . . . It was as if the sun went out! Close your eyes to see how dark it was . . . Oh, it was so dark nobody could see a thing!

"Will you let them go?" . . . "NO! NO! NO!"

(PLAGUE #10: DEATH OF THE FIRSTBORN)

OK, everyone sit down. At last God just shook his head. He was so angry with those people—and sad too. That night, one child from each family in Egypt died, but God kept all the Israelites safe. God didn't let them get hurt. And after that, when Moses asked if they could leave, the king told him, "Go! Go! Go!"

So let's try it one last time like that. Say, "Go! Go! Go!" "Will you let them go?" . . .
"GO! GO! GO!"

God's people left and everyone knew about the power of the Lord.

The end.

This would be a good story to tell with props. If you wish, gather pictures of the different types of plagues, or objects such as the ones listed below. Don't worry too much about the order of the plagues as you retell the story. That's not the vital part. Just make sure you end with the plague of the firstborn Egyptians dying.

PLAGUE:	PROP:
Water into Blood	Red Kool-Aid
Frogs	A plastic or rubber frog
Gnats	Bug repellent
Flies	A fly swatter
Dying livestock	A carton of milk
Sores on the people	Bandages
Hail	Baseballs or ice cubes
Locusts	A leaf that a grasshopper might eat
Darkness	A big black blanket
Death of firstborn Egyptians	A stuffed lamb (talk about Passover)

As you and a partner lead the following story, one of you reads or says the words while the other leads the actions. As each action is performed, the students will mirror the action back to you. Practice this story a few times before performing it to make sure the pace is smooth and the pauses are long enough. The empty spaces that appear after certain lines are simply there to break up the story and make it easier for you to find and keep your place.

THE MASTER OF DISASTER[4]
(a storymime version of "The Ten Plagues")

WHAT TO SAY:	WHAT TO DO:
Moses and Aaron went before the king.	Bow down with hands stretched out.
They said, "Let God's people go!"	Point off into the distance.
But the king just laughed.	Slap your leg and laugh.
"Who is this God? Why should I listen to him?"	Fold arms, look stern.
To prove God's power, Aaron threw down his stick.	Pretend to throw down a stick.
And it turned into a snake.	Look snaky and act slithery.
The king's magicians threw down their sticks.	Pretend to throw down more sticks.
They turned into snakes, too.	Look snaky and act slithery.
But Aaron's snake ate the other snakes!	Pretend to swallow, smile, and rub your tummy.
But still, the king wouldn't let God's people go.	Put your hands on your hips, shake your head no.
Then Moses and Aaron turned the river water into blood—	Make a disgusted face.
And the river stank.	Hold your nose.
But the king wouldn't let God's people go.	Put your hands on your hips, shake your head no.
Then God sent frogs,	Hop like a frog.

30 Old Testament Interactive Stories for Young Children

And flies,	Buzz like a fly.
Sick cows,	Hold your stomach and look like you're going to throw up.
And big ugly blisters . . . that really itched.	Scratch yourself and look sore.
Then God sent hail.	Put your hands up to cover your head.
With lots of lightning;	Pretend that your finger is lightning and strike the person next to you.
It even knocked down the trees!	Take one arm and tip it over like a falling tree. Yell, "Timber!"
And each time Moses stopped the plagues . . .	Put your hand out like you're a police officer stopping traffic.
When the king asked him to.	Fold your hands and pretend to plead.
But still the king wouldn't let God's people go.	Put your hands on your hips, shake your head no.
Then, God sent grasshoppers that hopped all over the place,	Go crazy, hopping all over.
And even chewed up all the crops.	Pretend to chew on corn-on-the-cob.
Then God sent a wind that blew the grasshoppers away.	Blow really hard at the person next to you.
Then, God sent darkness.	Close your eyes and feel around like you're standing in the dark.
But still, the king wouldn't let God's people go!	Put your hands on your hips, shake your head no.
Finally, God said, "There'll be one more disaster."	Hold one finger up high in the air.
"Tell the Israelites to paint their doorframes—	Pretend to dip a paintbrush and paint a doorframe.
With the blood of a lamb."	Make sheep ears on your head with your hands and say "baa."
And so that night, while the Egyptians were asleep . . .	Put your head against your hands, pretending to sleep.
God sent his mighty angel . . .	Draw a sword and hold it in front of you.
Who killed the firstborn Egyptians.	Swing your sword around and poke it forward.
Every house in Egypt was filled with sad people.	Make a sad face and pretend to cry.
But the Israelites slept safe and sound.	Put your head against your hands, pretending to sleep.
Finally, the king said, "Get out of here! I never want to see any of you again!"	Point off into the distance.
As the Israelites left, the Egyptians gave them their gold . . .	Pretend to bounce a bag of gold coins in your hand.
Their fancy earrings . .	Grab your earlobe and show it off to the person next to you.
And even their clothes!	Put your hands in front of you and cover yourself as if you're naked!
And God led his people through the desert . . .	Pretend to wipe sweat from your brow.
Just as he had promised Moses at the burning bush.	Hold out your hands in front of you and warm them as if you were in front of a campfire.
The end.	Bow and take a seat.

Summary

The plagues came
And the people of Egypt
Were very, very sad.
Some of the plagues
Hurt the people
And made them feel bad.

But the king
Wouldn't listen to Moses
And he wouldn't let them go.
Instead he just said
Over and over,
"No, no, no!"

But finally,
In the end when
So many children died,
The stubborn king
Nodded his head,
As he cried and cried and cried.

"Go!" he said,
"Go far away!
And never come back again!
I want these plagues
To stop for good
I want these plagues to end!"

At last God's people
Could leave the land
And they started on their way.
Praising God
For the freedom that
He'd given them on that day.

Chapter 9

The Israelites Cross the Red Sea

BASED ON:	Exodus 14
BIG IDEA:	When it seemed that they were trapped between the Egyptian army and the Red Sea, God rescued his people by parting the waters so they could cross over to safety.
BACKGROUND:	After granting permission for the Israelites to leave Egypt, Pharaoh changed his mind. He moved out with his army to recapture his slaves and cornered them at the Red Sea.
	When the people began to lose hope, Moses encouraged them to trust in God. Then God parted the waters of the Red Sea, allowing the Israelites to cross. When the Egyptians tried to follow, they were washed away. God had miraculously delivered his people.
KEY VERSE:	"Moses answered the people, 'Do not be afraid. Stand firm and you will see the deliverance the LORD will bring you today. The Egyptians you see today you will never see again. The LORD will fight for you; you need only to be still'" (Exodus 14:13, 14).

This is one of the most famous Bible stories, so if your children have been attending church for a while, they've probably heard it before.

When you tell it, emphasize God's deliverance and guidance for the Israelites rather than his judgment and wrath against the Egyptians.

Use the following imaginary journey to help the children picture the Israelites walking through the desert. When leading an imaginary journey, remember to accept whatever suggestions your children offer, no matter how silly. Find a way to work their ideas into the story!

Kids, let's pretend that we are no longer in this room, but that we are in the middle of a desert! We're walking through the desert . . . walking through the desert . . . Can you feel the hot sun? . . . Are you hot and thirsty? Show me how hot you are! . . .

Can you think of any things we might see in this desert? . . . *(Accept whatever the children suggest. Following are some examples of what might be said and how you could use each idea.)* **. . . Yes! There might be cactuses in the desert! Careful! We're walking through a bunch of cactuses! Tiptoe . . . tiptoe . . . tiptoe . . . Don't bump into a cactus! . . . Don't sit on a cactus! . . . Ouch!**

What else might we see in this desert? Yes! Lizards! There might be lizards in this desert! Look around . . . Do you see any lizards? Where are they? Run away from the lizards! . . . *(as you demonstrate, run in place so the children will not scatter throughout the room)* **. . . Run! . . . Don't let the lizards nibble on your toesies!**

Whew! We got away from those lizards! That's great. Now, we need to climb up over this sand dune . . . It's a little slippery because it's made out of sand! . . . Don't tumble all the way back down! We need to get to the top. . . . We made it! Hurray!

(Look off to the side of the room.) **Oh, my! What's that? I see something very strange up ahead! It's a tall cloud going all the way up from the ground to the sky! And it's moving through the desert! It's blocking out some of the sun! So it's not so hot anymore! That's nice . . . Ah . . . it's cooling off . . . But what's this? Who are all those people? . . . Kids, let's sit down and see if we can find out what's going on out here in this desert!**

Many times you can use a monologue or a skit to follow an imaginary journey. Another technique is to interview another teacher (or teen volunteer) who plays the part of one of the people in the story. Listed below is a sample of how an interview might sound if you were interviewing one of the Israelites in this story. Consider having the Israelite wear a robe or another simple costume.

Teacher:	**Um, excuse me.**
Israelite:	*(Entering the room, in a hurry)* **Yes, yes, what do you want?**
Teacher:	**Um, where are you going in such a hurry?**
Israelite:	**It's the Egyptians! They're chasing us!**
Teacher:	**But why? Why would they do that?**
Israelite:	**We used to be their slaves. But then Moses came and God used ten terrible disasters to show everyone in the land that he is the one true God. Finally they told us to leave.**
Teacher:	**But if they told you to leave, why are they chasing you?**
Israelite:	**They changed their minds! Now they want to kill us or turn us into slaves again!**
Teacher:	**But what are you going to do?**
Israelite:	**I don't know! See that cloud over there?**
Teacher:	**Yes, it was giving us shade from the sun.**
Israelite:	**Well, God sent that cloud to lead us and protect us. But look where the cloud is going!**
Teacher:	*(Peering off in the distance)* **Toward the ocean?**
Israelite:	**That's the Red Sea! We'll be trapped! I don't understand why God would lead us here! It doesn't make any sense!**
Teacher:	**Well maybe he's got something exciting planned.**
Israelite:	**Who knows? Look, I can't talk anymore; the Egyptians are coming! I have to go.** *(Hurrying offstage)*
Teacher:	*(Calling after the Israelite)* **Be safe! Be careful!** *(Turning to the children)* **Boy, I really hope she'll be OK. I hope God helps them. Otherwise the Egyptians just might get 'em!**

If you have a team of teachers, this would be a good place to have another teacher come forward to lead the next activity. If you're like many teachers, it's just you! If so, that's fine. Hand out blue streamers, ribbons, or scarves.

Ok, kids! I want you to be the waves on the sea! Move your streamers up and down to make waves! Let's see some big waves . . . and some small ones . . . Good! . . . Is it windy out on the Red Sea today? . . . Wow! I guess it is! . . . But look! Now Moses is praying to God and holding up his shepherd's staff! And now, the waves are moving to the side! *(Walk down the center of the students, encouraging them to step to the side to form a pathway down the middle of the room.)*

There's a pathway for God's people! *(Have the children who are bordering the pathway hold the ends of their streamers in each hand to form the pathway, all the rest of the kids can keep waving their streamers.)*

And guess what! God's people got across safely! Hurray!

But look! . . . Now the Egyptians are coming! They're chasing the Israelites! . . . But do you know what God is going to do to stop them? . . . That's right! All you kids forming the pathway, and everyone else, run around—the path is gone! Let's have Red Sea waves everywhere in the room!

Let the children run around for a while, then corral them back together and have them hand in their streamers. Then, after they're calmed down, explain that God's people were safe on the other side of the Red Sea and they were so happy they sang and danced!

Sing the following song to close the lesson. Teach the children simple actions that relate to each verse!

RED SEA WAVES
(sing to the tune of "London Bridge")

Red Sea waves are piled high,
Piled high,
Piled high!
Red Sea waves are piled high,
For God's people!

They are walking on the path,
On the path,
On the path!
They are walking on the path,
Through the Red Sea!

Safely to the other side!
Other side,
Other side!
Safely to the other side,
God has saved them!

Red Sea waves are crashing down,
Crashing down,
Crashing down!
Red Sea waves are crashing down,
On the Egyptians!

They are floating far away!
Far away,
Far away!
They are floating far away,
From God's people!

Summary

Waves on the shore,
Waves piled high,
So Moses and his friends could walk on by.

But the waves came down,
With a crashing sound,
When the king and his men walked upon the ground.

Chapter 10

Moses Brings God's Ten Rules

BASED ON: Exodus 32, 33

BIG IDEA: Even though they turned from God to worship a golden calf, God was willing to forgive the Israelites and stick with his people because of his friendship with Moses.

BACKGROUND: After God delivered the children of Israel from slavery in Egypt, it didn't take them long to forget about God and falter in their allegiance to him. After Moses had been gone for a long time up in the mountains receiving God's laws, the people became bored and restless. They pressured Aaron into making them a golden cow to worship.

  Both God and Moses were furious with the people for their idolatry, and there were severe consequences for the idolaters. Yet because of his deep love for Moses God didn't abandon his people.

KEY VERSE: "The LORD said to Moses, 'Go down, because your people, whom you brought up out of Egypt, have become corrupt. They have been quick to turn away from what I commanded them and have made themselves an idol cast in the shape of a calf'" (Exodus 32:7, 8).

Young children are used to having rules. They have rules at home, rules at daycare or preschool, and rules at church. Be careful when you tell this story to emphasize that God gave his rules as a guide for the people, or as a way to show them how much they needed his daily love and forgiveness (see Romans 3:20), but not as a way to earn their way into Heaven.

Explain that you're going to do a special story in which the whole class can help you by putting on pretend masks! **"Boys and girls, reach behind your back and grab the bag of pretend masks that I put back there earlier today. Now, let's practice for this story. Whatever mask I put on, put the same mask on!"**

Pick up an imaginary mask and put it on your face. Cover your face with your hands. Then, when you pull your hands away, make a huge happy face. Put your hands up to cover your face to take off the mask. Then put the next mask on. Put on a sad face, then an angry one, then a surprised face. Have fun with it.

Then, introduce the story. **"OK! Great! Let's all start out with our normal faces, without any masks on."** (The underlined words below are your cues for the "masks.")

> **When Moses left to get God's laws for the people, the people were <u>happy</u>! . . . But when he didn't come back for a long time, they were <u>sad.</u> . . . They told Aaron to make them a statue of cow to worship, and he was <u>surprised</u>! . . .**
>
> **Meanwhile, Moses was on the mountain getting God's laws and Moses was <u>happy</u>! . . . But the Lord showed him that the people were praying to the statue and Moses was <u>surprised</u> . . . and <u>angry</u>!**
>
> **Moses went down the mountain. When the people saw him they were <u>surprised</u>! . . . And Moses was <u>mad.</u> . . . Then Moses took away the golden statue and some of the bad people were <u>mad,</u> . . . but some of the good people were <u>sad,</u> . . . because they knew what they'd done was wrong.**
>
> **And even though God was <u>angry</u> with them, . . . he didn't leave his people alone in the desert. That made them <u>happy</u> . . . to have a God who would give them a second chance.**
>
> **The end.**

As an interlude between this first story and the second, you may wish to sing this song a few times *(sung to the tune of* "Are You Sleeping?"*)*, and then read the poem.

God gave Moses
> *(students repeat, "God gave Moses")*

Two big stones!
> *(students repeat)*

With the Ten Commandments,
> *(students repeat)*

For their lives.
> *(students repeat)*

> God gave 10 Commandments as a guide for our lives,[5]
> So here's how to act until he arrives:
>
> 1. Only worship the true God, the one God alone,
> 2. Don't ever make idols of plastic or stone.
> 3. Use God's name with honor and use it with care,
> 4. Take one day a week for worship and prayer.
> 5. Always honor your parents. Respect and obey 'em.
> 6. Don't harm other people or murder or slay 'em!
> 7. Be loyal in marriage, avoiding affairs;
> 8. Don't steal things from others or take what is theirs.
> 9. Don't lie or deceive or say things that aren't true.
> 10. And don't scheme to get what's not given to you.
>
> Should you keep 'em?
> Yes, keep 'em! And carry 'em around!
> In your heart. In your head. They should always be found.
> But why should you keep 'em?
> What good does it do?
> It's a way to show thanks for what God's done for you!

Kids, let's act out this story! It'll be fun!

Ok, let's pretend that we're Moses and we're climbing up the mountain to talk to God. . . . We have to climb really high . . . higher . . . higher! . . . Wow! We sure are high up on this mountain! Is it cold up here? . . . Is there snow?! . . . Make a snowball, but don't throw it at me!

Then God gave Moses two big rocks with his rules written on them. . . . Pick up the rocks . . . they're really big . . . they're really heavy. . . . Don't drop 'em on your toe!

Now, we have to climb down the mountain carrying the heavy rocks! . . . Step carefully . . . Don't fall . . .

Oh, no! I just looked down the mountain and saw God's people praying to a golden statue of a cow! . . . That makes me mad! . . . Are you mad too? . . . Show me how mad you are. . . . Throw down the rocks! Throw them so hard they smash on the ground! . . .

Now, let's smash up that golden cow! . . . Karate kick the cow! . . . We should worship God, not statues! Moses ground that cow up until it was just a little pile of sand! . . . Chop it up into tiny pieces!

Now, let's pretend we're Moses praying to God to rescue the people. . . . Do you think God will listen to our prayer?

He does! Hooray! . . . Let's lift our hands up and praise God for still loving his people even though they were naughty!

The end.

Summary

The people made a cow
Out of shiny, shiny gold.
And they prayed and they bowed
Even though they'd been told
Not to do such a thing,
Not to worship what they'd made.
Still the people made a cow
And they bowed and they prayed.

Moses wasn't happy
And he got really mad
'Cause the people kept on doing
All the things they knew were bad.
So then Moses prayed to God
And he listened to his prayer.
And the Lord forgave his people
But he said, "Beware!
Stay away from sin,
Don't worship what is made!
For if you worship me instead
You need never be afraid."

Chapter 11

Snakes in the Desert

BASED ON: Numbers 21:4-9

BIG IDEA: When snakes infested the camp of the rebellious Israelites, God reminded the people that only he could save them.

BACKGROUND: While traveling through the desert, God's people became impatient. They complained to God that they didn't have enough food and water and that they didn't like the manna and quail he was providing for them.

As a result, God allowed venomous snakes to come into their camp and many people died. Only then did the people admit their sin and turn to the Lord. God told Moses to make a bronze snake and put it on a pole. If the people bitten by snakes looked at the bronze snake, they would live. In this way, God reminded them of his power and protection.

KEY VERSE: "The LORD said to Moses, 'Make a snake and put it up on a pole; anyone who is bitten can look at it and live'" (Numbers 21:8).

As you tell this story, be careful not to portray God as vindictive or mean, sending poisonous snakes to kill people like some kind of cosmic bully. God is both just and merciful. Sometimes his holy justice is frightening, but his mercy is always freeing.

Get some clay or modeling clay and practice the following story a couple of times before telling it to your students. Add your own ideas!

Long ago, God's people were walking through the wilderness. They walked past lots of rocks.	Form the clay into a ball.
Some were big and some were small.	Break up the clay into little balls.
But the people became angry with God. They wanted different food!	Ball up the clay and pretend to take a bite out of it.
Not rocks—yuck!	Make a nasty face.
They remembered back to what it was like in Egypt, before God parted the Red Sea.	Break the ball apart into two halves.
So they complained to God. And God was angry about all their complaining!	Ball it together and smash the clay flat with your fist…
He felt like smushing 'em, but he didn't.	Begin rolling it into a snake.
Instead he let some deadly snakes come into their campsite!	Hold up the snake. Slither it at the kids.
The snakes bit the people	Make the snake bite you.
and many people died!	Stick out your tongue.
Everyone was very sad.	Make the snake into a frowny face.
So the people were sorry for complaining to God and they cried.	Form the clay into a teardrop and make it fall from your eye.
They asked Moses to pray for them. God told Moses to build a pole	Begin breaking it in half and rolling out the halves. Straighten out one rolled piece of clay.
and wrap a bronze snake around it.	Wrap the second piece of clay around the first to form the snake on the pole.

Then, when the snakes bit the people, if the people <u>looked at the pole</u> with the metal snake on it they wouldn't die.	Wave the pole in front of the children.
And everyone was <u>happy and thankful</u> to God again. The end.	Roll them together and form a smile.

If you're emphasizing how God's Spirit led the Israelites through the desert, you could play a game of follow the leader. Tell part of the story to the students and then have them all get up and follow you to a new spot to continue the story. Walk to a variety of places as you tell the story little by little. Give the cloud person a pillow to carry and the pillar of fire person a candle. Then, let them lead you wherever they desire around the classroom or church property. Continue the story at each new place. Take turns being the leaders. Explain that the cloud led the people by day and the fire by night. Turn the lights on and off and follow the appropriate leader.

You could also teach the children to say the following four phrases during the story as you tell it: "I'm hungry!", "I'm thirsty!", "Are we there yet?", "I gotta go to the bathroom!" After each part, you could say Moses' line, "You guys are a bunch of whiners. Just trust in God and he'll provide!"

Then sing either of the following simple songs, or make up your own words to a popular tune your children know!

ARE YOU HISSING?
(To the tune of "Are You Sleeping?")
Are you hissing?
Are you hissing?
Little snake, little snake,
Do you want to bite me?
Do you want to bite me?
And make me ache?
Make me ache?

SLITHER, SLITHER LITTLE SNAKE
(To the tune of "Twinkle, Twinkle, Little Star")
Slither, slither little snake,
Do not bite me by mistake.
Stay away and don't come near!
Do not bite me on the ear!
Slither, slither little snake.
Do not bite me by mistake.

Kids, let's act out this story!

First, I want you to pretend to be those people looking down at the snakes coming! Oh, no! They're scary snakes! Ready?! Go! . . . And freeze!

Next, let's become those slithering snakes! Get ready to slither all over the ground. Ready? And slither! . . . Pretend to bite one of the Israelites! . . . Yikes! Freeze!

OK, those people were sad because of the snakes. Let's become those sad people. Ready? Go! . . . And freeze!

The people asked Moses to pray to God. And God told him to make a tall pole and put a metal snake on it. Let's build the pole . . . Good! And now, let's put a metal snake on it . . . Nicely done! And freeze!

So then, when the snakes bit the people, if the people looked at the pole, they would be OK. Everyone pretend that you just got bitten by a snake! . . . Did the snake bite your toe? . . . Your leg? . . . Does it hurt really bad? . . . Look up! Will God heal us? Yes! Are you OK now? . . . Yeah! Let's all jump around and praise God because he's strong enough to heal his people!

The end!

Summary

Snakes in the sand and snakes on the ground,
Snakes in the desert slithering around.
The people didn't like it or think it was right.
'Cause when the snakes came slithering,
      The snakes began to bite!

"Owie!" said a person
Whose foot was feeling sore.
"I wish these snakes would go away
And not come back no more!"

But then the people told Moses
They were sorry for their pouting
And Moses prayed
      And God forgave
           Their fussing and their shouting.
Then Moses made a metal snake and put it on a pole,
And everyone who looked at it was healed up and whole.

Chapter 12

Balaam Argues with a Donkey

BASED ON: Numbers 22–24

BIG IDEA: God used Balaam, a sorcerer, to bless his people. God can use anyone to accomplish his purposes, even an unbeliever.

BACKGROUND: Fear of the Israelites had spread throughout Moab. The king decided to call on a famous sorcerer named Balaam to curse the Israelites. Even though Balaam showed evidence of real faith, he was in the sorcery business to make a living and was more concerned about making a quick buck than about honoring the living God.

KEY VERSE: "The donkey said to Balaam, 'Am I not your own donkey, which you have always ridden, to this day? Have I been in the habit of doing this to you?'
      'No,' he said.
      Then the LORD opened Balaam's eyes, and he saw the angel of the LORD standing in the road with his sword drawn. So he bowed low and fell facedown" (Numbers 22:30, 31).

Balaam the sorcerer didn't trust in the Lord, but he did acknowledge the power of Israel's God. He was willing to obey God as long as it was in his own best interests—as long as he could profit from it. This story reminds us that our obedience to God should grow from our love for God and our faith in him rather than our desire for personal gain.

Since this story may be unfamiliar to some of the younger children, you may wish to have them simply sit and listen to you read or tell it all the way through before you tell it in an interactive way. (Of course, feel free to have the students join along with all or part of the refrain!)

Once long ago there was a wizard named Balaam. He knew about the Lord, but worshiped other made-up gods too.

One day, a king sent some men to ask him to say bad things about God's people (those bad things are called *curses*). But he wouldn't do it because he didn't think God would be happy. But later, he changed his mind when he thought about how much money the men would pay him.

So, he hopped onto his donkey and followed the men. Now this is where the story gets really interesting! Because . . .

As Balaam rode his donkey he didn't have a clue;
Why the donkey stopped doing what he told it to do.
It went off the path.
So he gave it a WHACK!
Until his donkey did as it was told!

Now, was that a very kind way to treat the donkey? . . . No, it wasn't. But what Balaam didn't know was that the donkey went off the road because it was afraid of God's angel standing in the path with a big sharp sword!

So they went a little further and soon they came to a narrow path between two stone walls . . .

As Balaam rode his donkey he didn't have a clue;
Why the donkey stopped doing what he told it to do.
It smushed his foot
So he gave it a WHACK!
Until his donkey did as it was told!

Once again the donkey had seen the angel, and it was scared! Then the angel went ahead of them and waited. Soon, Balaam came riding up on his donkey . . .

As Balaam rode his donkey he didn't have a clue;
Why the donkey stopped doing what he told it to do.
It sat in the path
So he gave it a WHACK!
But still it wouldn't do as it was told!

Then, the strangest thing of all happened. God let the donkey talk! And it said, "Why did you hit me three times?"
And Balaam said, "You're making me look like a fool!"
And the donkey said, "You're doing that all by yourself, big guy!" Well, it didn't say that *exactly*, but it did say, "Haven't I always been a good donkey?"
Balaam had to agree.
Then God let Balaam see the angel with the sword, and he was scared! The angel told him that the donkey had saved him by stopping because God was angry that he was planning to say curses. Then Balaam promised to say only what God told him to say.
The end.

If you wish to transition immediately into the next activity, say something like this, "Hmm . . . we still don't know if Balaam is going to say good things about God's people or bad things! We still don't know if he's going to keep his promise to God! But before we find out, let's have a little fun and act out this story!"

I'm going to teach you something to say and something special to do when I tell the story! When I say <u>donkey</u> we'll all turn our hands into donkey ears and say, "Hee haw! Hee haw! Owie, owie ouch!" Let's try it! "HEE HAW! HEE HAW! OWIE, OWIE OUCH!"
And whenever I talk about the <u>angel</u> we'll stand big and strong and hold out our swords and say, "I'm on God's side!" Ready, let's practice: "I'M ON GOD'S SIDE!" And finally, whenever I talk about <u>Balaam</u>, we'll make an angry face and say, "I'll get you, Mr. Donkey!" . . . "I'LL GET YOU, MR. DONKEY!"
OK, let's start the story!

Once long ago there was a man who would do almost anything to make lots of money. His name was Balaam . . . *(I'll get you, Mr. Donkey!)*
One day he was going to say bad things about God's people. He was riding on his donkey. . . . *(Hee haw! Hee haw! Owie, owie ouch!)*
But suddenly, even though he didn't see it, God sent his angel . . . *(I'm on God's side!)* . . . It stood right in their path! And just then, the donkey . . . *(Hee haw! Hee haw! Owie, owie ouch!)* . . . walked off the path! So then it got whacked by Balaam! . . . *(I'll get you, Mr. Donkey!)*
They went on their way. Soon, they were going by a wall. Once again, right in front of them stood the angel! . . . *(I'm on God's side!)* . . . And the donkey . . . *(Hee haw! Hee haw! Owie, owie ouch!)* . . . moved to the side, smushing Baalam's foot! . . . *(I'll get you, Mr. Donkey!)* . . . So once again he beat the donkey! . . . *(Hee-haw! Hee haw! Owie, owie ouch!)*
For a third time, God sent his angel . . . *(I'm on God's side!)* . . . who held out his sword.

And this time, the donkey . . . *(Hee-haw! Hee haw! Owie, owie ouch!)* . . . **just stopped and sat down! Well, when that happened, that guy named Balaam** . . . *(I'll get you, Mr. Donkey!)* . . . **beat it *even more* until finally, God let him see what his pet had been seeing all along—that great big angel. . . .** *(I'm on God's side!)*

And after talking to him, that man agreed to do whatever God said. The end!

Explain that Balaam remembered his promise, and every time the king told him to say something bad about God's people, he ended up saying something good over and over again until the bad king couldn't stand it anymore! You can celebrate God's blessings on his people by inviting the children to join you in this chant!

Good things, good things, never bad!
Make God's people really glad!
Good things, good things, never bad!
Make God's people really glad!

Summary

Balaam and his donkey . . . donkey . . . donkey . . .
Balaam and his donkey went walking down the road.

But the donkey stopped walking . . . walking . . . walking . . .
The donkey stopped walking down the desert road.

So Balaam hit the donkey . . . donkey . . . donkey . . .
Balaam hit the donkey who'd stopped walking down the road.

Once again they went walking . . . walking . . . walking . . .
Again they went walking down the desert road.

But the donkey kept stopping . . . stopping . . . stopping . . .
The donkey kept stopping on the desert road!

So Balaam hit the donkey . . . donkey . . . donkey . . .
Balaam hit the donkey who'd stopped walking down the road.

Then the donkey started talking . . . talking . . . talking . . .
The donkey started talking on the desert road!

And Balaam saw the angel . . . angel . . . angel . . .
Balaam saw the angel on the desert road.

Then the angel started talking . . . talking . . . talking . . .
The angel started talking on the desert road!

And Balaam started listening . . . listening . . . listening . . .
Balaam started listening to the angel in the road.

And Balaam made a promise . . . a promise . . . a promise . . .
Balaam made a promise to do as he was told.

Chapter 13

Spying on the Promised Land

BASED ON: Numbers 13, 14

BIG IDEA: God's people refused to believe that he had given them the land, so they suffered severe consequences for their unbelief.

BACKGROUND: God had delivered his people from slavery, led them through the Red Sea, and guided them through the desert. They were on the brink of receiving all of the blessings God had promised them in a land "flowing with milk and honey."

        Following God's guidance, Moses sent one man from each tribe to explore the land God had promised to give them. However, ten of the spies brought back reports that only served to frighten and deter the Israelites from trusting in the Lord and taking over the land. As a result, God's people had to wander for 40 more years in the wilderness and none of the people, except for the two trusting spies, would be allowed to actually set foot in the Promised Land.

KEY VERSE: "And they spread among the Israelites a bad report about the land they had explored. They said, 'The land we explored devours those living in it. All the people we saw there are of great size'" (Numbers 13:32).

The central messages of this story are that we should trust in God's promises and that when we don't, we'll suffer the consequences of unbelief. You'll want to be sure you don't give the children the impression that if we obey good will happen, and if we disobey bad will happen. Sometimes good things happen to bad people and bad things happen to good people. Instead, you'll want to emphasize how important it is to trust God and follow the example of Joshua and Caleb rather than the example of the ten spies who didn't trust God.

Since the spies brought back a large cluster of grapes, you may wish to serve grape juice or have a snack of grapes for snack time.

Sometimes people shy away from using puppets because they don't feel skilled enough to open and close the puppet's mouth only at the appropriate times. You can solve this problem by not having the puppet say anything to the children, but instead just lean close and whisper things in your ear. Then, you can have the puppet nod or shake its head to answer questions that you ask it.

Remember to always keep your puppet moving, even when it's not talking. This will help create the illusion that the puppet is alive.

Practice the story a few times with your puppet to become comfortable with the interchanges between the two of you. The script below is just a sample to give you ideas. Don't feel like you need to memorize it. Instead, when you tell the story to the children, put the script aside and tell the story in your own words.

WHAT TO SAY:	SUGGESTED PUPPET ACTION:
Boys and girls, I want you to meet my friend. His name is *(insert the name of your puppet. I'll give you an example of how it could work)* **Fang the Wolf!**	As you introduce the puppet, pull it out of a box or crate and hold it on your lap. Remember to keep it moving!
(To the puppet) **So, Fang, you were there that day when God's people arrived in the land?**	Make your puppet nod.
Where were you?	Let the puppet whisper to you.
You were hiding in the forest!	Make your puppet nod.
So what happened?	Let the puppet whisper to you.

You're telling me Moses chose twelve men to be spies?	Nod.
And one wolf!	Nod.
Wait a minute, I don't think the Bible talks about any wolf being there, but let's say you were. Why did you follow them?	Whisper.
What! You wanted to eat them!?	Make your puppet nod enthusiastically.
Fang, are you sure?	Nod some more. Then, lean over to whisper to you.
You think they'd taste like chicken?!	Nod very enthusiastically.
Well, let's get back to the story. Tell me what the spies did.	Whisper.
Oh, you want to show me.	Nod.
OK, go ahead.	After you tell it to go ahead, move the puppet around, let it climb all over you, hide under your leg, peek out from behind your back, stuff like that. Have fun with it!
Wow! They did a lot of spying didn't they?	Nod.
And did you eat them?	Nod.
No you didn't! Now, when the spies saw all the tall strong men that lived in the land, how did they act?	Make your puppet hide its head under your arms.
Are you scared?	Shake his head "no."
Are you sure?	Shake his head "no."
Were they scared?	Nod lots and lots. Climb out of hiding.
So then when they returned, how many of the spies told the people to be scared?	Lean over to whisper to you.
Ten of them!	Nod.
Ten out of twelve spies?	Nod.
And how many told the people to trust God instead and go into the land?	Lean over to whisper to you.
Only two?	Nod.
What about you, Fang? Would you have trusted in God?	Nod.
Good, I'm proud of you. *(Hug your puppet)*	
Is there anything else?	Nod. Lean over to whisper to you.
No, Fang. I'm not going to let you eat me up! Maybe I can get you a hamburger instead. OK?	Nod.
Great. Kids, let's thank Fang for coming out today!	Make your puppet bow to the audience. Then, put it away again in the crate or box.

A fun way to encourage children to participate in a story is to have them make louder and then softer sounds as you direct them, like the director of a choir or a band. **"OK, kids, I want you to make some special sounds during this story to help me tell it. I'll raise my hand when I want you to make the sounds louder, and I'll lower my hand when I want you to make them softer. Let's practice with the sound of a cow. Ready?"**

Hold your hand up high, then slowly lower it. Raise it up a little, then lower it again. Try it a little faster, then slowly again. The children will start to have fun with it.

You could use different items for directing the students. For example, use a director's stick, a rubber chicken, or even a toilet plunger to direct them!

Each time you start your lines, begin with your hand in the middle of the air.

WHAT TO SAY:	SUGGESTED ACTION:
Moses and God's people were in the wilderness. There were wolves. Howl like wolves everyone . . .	Raise or lower your hand as desired to make the audience louder or softer.
And growling bears . . .	
And maybe a bunch of frogs . . .	
Well, Moses sent 12 men to spy out the land God had promised them. They went at night and heard the owls hooting . . .	
And the wind blowing . . .	
And the crickets chirping and chattering in the shadows . . .	
Sometimes the owls were really loud!	Raise your hand high.
And sometimes they were really quiet.	Lower your hand.
Sometimes the frogs were really loud!	Raise your hand high.
And sometimes they were really quiet.	Lower your hand.
Well, the twelve men went up in the hills to spy out the land. They saw giants who acted really mean . . .	Raise your hand.
I mean, really mean . . .	Raise your hand higher.
Really, really mean! . . .	Raise your hand even higher.
Then the spies snuck past the seashore and it was very quiet, except for a few gulls calling out over the waves . . .	Lower your hand.
The spies could hear the waves washing gently against the sand . . .	Keep it low. Raise it up and down a little.
But sometimes, the waves went crashing against the shore! . . .	Way high!
Then, the spies came to a valley and grabbed some fruit that was so heavy it took two guys to carry it! They were grunting really loudly! . . .	Way high!
When they got back to Moses and the Israelites, the people were glad to see them! Some people shouted! . . .	Way high!
Others just waved . . .	Low.
Most of the spies were scared of those giants! They told the people how scary the giants were and the people cried! . . .	Middle.
Some cried a little . . .	Low.
But most of them cried a lot! . . .	High.
Then one of the spies, named Caleb, told the people to be quiet, and they were.	Start high, get low.
He said God would help them win, but the people just started crying again . . .	Start in the middle, get higher.
Moses and Aaron told them to trust God, but they cried even louder! . . .	Really high.
Finally, God told the people they wouldn't be able to enter the special land yet, because they hadn't trusted in him. Some people were quiet, but others were really sad . . .	Start low, get high.
And for a long time they had to walk through the desert where there were snakes . . .	Low.
Lots of snakes . . .	Middle.
Even more snakes! . . .	High.
And it wasn't until many years later that God's people were able to go into the land.	
And when they were finally able to enter it, they were very, very happy and thankful to God. I think they cheered for God . . .	Super high.
The end!	Bow to the audience.

For a simple craft project consider having the children make spy telescopes out of paper towel rolls.

Summary

The sneaky spies were quite surprised
When they saw the people there.
For all those guys were giant-sized,
So they couldn't help but stare!
"We're small," they thought.
"They'll stomp us all. We just don't have a chance!"
(I'd say they were so terrified they almost wet their pants!)

Just two of those spies trusted in God
And told the folks to go.
"We'll take this land by his mighty hand!
For the Lord has told us so!"

But the people were scared and doubted God
And began to shake and cry.
"We can't go there!" they said,
"For if we do, we know we'll die!"

And that made God so angry
That he made them all return
To the hot and sticky desert
Where the sun just loved to burn.

So the people had to walk around
That desert 'til they died.
Because they hadn't trusted God
To lead and be their guide.

Chapter 14

Jericho's Walls Fall Over

BASED ON: Joshua 6:12-21

BIG IDEA: God knocked down the walls of Jericho and gave the Israelites a great victory on their quest to conquer the Promised Land.

BACKGROUND: The Israelites had been wandering around in the desert for years and years. Forty years earlier, they'd approached the Promised Land, but because of their unbelief, God had made them wander in the desert.

A new generation of Israelites grew up and, after a miraculous crossing of the Jordan River at flood stage (reminiscent of the crossing of the Red Sea), the people entered the Promised Land. The time had come to believe God's promise that he would hand the land over to his people.

Jericho was an ancient city that had stood for thousands of years. Many people thought it was invincible. It had walls that were up to 20 feet thick and more than 20 feet tall, so when God led Joshua and the children of Israel into the Promised Land, one of the first tasks was to conquer Jericho. God's unusual battle strategy proved to everyone (including the Israelites) that God was powerful enough to deliver them from any enemy!

KEY VERSE: "When the trumpets sounded, the people shouted, and at the sound of the trumpet, when the people gave a loud shout, the wall collapsed; so every man charged straight in, and they took the city" (Joshua 6:20).

As you tell this popular story, be sure to make it clear to your children that it was God's power, not the shouting or the marching of the Israelites, that knocked down Jericho's walls. The people were simply obedient to God and trusted him to fight against the city in his own way. And when they obeyed him, God did something amazing!

You could easily use props to retell this story. Use army men, action figures, a kazoo, and some boxes or building blocks.

The city of Jericho had tall walls *(build the walls with the boxes or blocks)*. **The leader of God's people was a man named Joshua!** *(hold up one of the action figures)*. **And he told them to follow God's advice and God would knock over the walls of Jericho!** *(build the wall out of boxes of blocks)*

So, Joshua and the people marched around the city like God told them *(be silly and march "Joshua" around the city)*. **The people of Jericho watched and laughed from the top of the walls** *(make the army men laugh and dance around)*. **This happened every day for a whole week. Joshua leading his people** *(march "Joshua" around the city)*, **and the soldiers of Jericho laughing at them as they passed** *(make the army men jump around and laugh)*. **Day after day for six days** *(make them do it a bunch of times, really quickly)* . . . . **Until finally, on the last day they blew their trumpets!** *(pull out the kazoo)*.

When the trumpets sounded the people shouted as loud as they could—why don't you do that part? Ready, the people shouted as loud as they could . . . I said as loud as they could! . . .

Good job!

And the walls fell down! *(knock them down)* **and God's people knocked over all the people of Jericho!** *(make your action figure attack all the little green army men)*

God fought for his people and they listened to God!

The end.

Another fun way to tell this story would be to act it out, marching around "Jericho" with the children. Pretend that a desk in the middle of the room is the city of Jericho and then tiptoe around the desk as you chant this together:

"On Monday . . .
(tiptoe around the "city")
Shh . . . they were quiet as they walked around the walls.
Shh . . . they were quiet and they didn't speak at all.
Shh . . . they were quiet as they did what God had said.
Shh . . . they were quiet as they climbed into their beds . . . "
(Everyone lies down and pretends to sleep)
"Then, they snored . . .
And they snored . . .
And they slept 'til the morning light . . . "
(Sit up, yawn, stand up, and say . . .)

"On Tuesday . . .
(tiptoe around the "city")
Shh . . . they were quiet as they walked around the walls.
Shh . . . they were quiet and they didn't speak at all.
Shh . . . they were quiet as they did what God had said.
Shh . . . they were quiet as they climbed into their beds . . ."
(Everyone lies down and pretends to sleep)
"Then, they snored . . .
And they snored . . .
And they slept 'til the morning light . . ."
(Sit up, yawn, stand up and say . . .)

"On Wednesday . . .
(tiptoe around the "city")
And so on.

Go through the marching and chanting and sleeping for Wednesday, Thursday, Friday, and Saturday. Then, on Sunday say,

"On Sunday . . .
(tiptoe around the "city")
Shh . . . they were quiet as they walked around the walls.
Shh . . . they were quiet and they didn't speak at all.
Shh . . . they were quiet 'til the seventh time around.
THEN THEY SHOUTED AND THEY SHOUTED AND THE WALLS FELL DOWN!
Let's all shout like God's people! . . .
Hooray! . . .
God knocked over those walls and everyone in the land knew the Lord really was leading his people!

You could, of course, also sing the old campfire song, "Joshua Fought the Battle of Jericho!" and act out the words to the song as you sing it.

Summary

The walls of Jericho were tall
And, oh, those walls were thick!
So other armies felt real small.
And very scared and sick.
For no one could break down those walls
That were so tall and strong
        (Until, that is, when Joshua
        And God's people came along!)

Joshua led the people
In a march around the town.
Step by step by step they walked;
And didn't make a sound.
Each day they marched in silence,
Until one week was through.
And then they shouted really loud
Because God told them to.

And suddenly the people heard
A rumble and a tumble
And all those walls around the town
Began to crack and crumble!
Yes, God had broken down the walls;
His people won the war.
And the Lord became more famous
Than he'd ever been before!

Chapter 15

Gideon Fights the Midianites

BASED ON: Judges 6, 7

BIG IDEA: Even though Gideon wasn't experienced as a leader, God chose him and gifted him for a specific purpose. God gifts us to serve him, too.

BACKGROUND: For seven years the Midianites had been oppressing the Israelites. They destroyed the Israelite herds, flocks, and crops. Finally, when the Israelites called out to the Lord, the angel of the Lord appeared to timid Gideon and called on him to lead God's people to freedom.

KEY VERSE: "The three companies blew the trumpets and smashed the jars. Grasping the torches in their left hands and holding in their right hands the trumpets they were to blow, they shouted, 'A sword for the LORD and for Gideon!' While each man held his position around the camp, all the Midianites ran, crying out as they fled" (Judges 7:20, 21).

Gideon's story includes the accounts of the fleece without dew and then with dew, of the men kneeling to drink like dogs, and so on. Some of these details might make the story a little too complex, confusing, or convoluted for younger children. For that reason I've left them out.

When you tell the story, focus on the main struggles of Gideon overcoming his fear and trusting in the Lord, and the people finally finding freedom as God miraculously delivered them from their enemies.

Practice reading or telling the following story once or twice aloud before doing it in front of the children.

WHAT TO SAY:	SUGGESTED SOUND / ACTION:
The Israelites had turned away from God and worshiped false gods . . .	"Naughty, naughty, naughty!"
So the Lord let the people of Midian take over. The Israelites had to run away and hide in caves!	"They'll never find us here!"
When they planted crops, the Midianites took the food away.	"Bummer, dude!"
So finally, they prayed to God for help and God sent an angel to talk to Gideon. "Hello, mighty warrior!" said the angel.	"Hello, mighty warrior!"
At first Gideon didn't know it was God's angel.	"Huh? Who are you?"
He doubted God would really help them, but then God's angel touched a rock with a stick and fire jumped out of the rock!	"Ta-da!"
Then, the angel disappeared!	"Whoa."
Gideon was scared,	*Bite your fingernails.*
But God told him to trust in the Lord instead.	*Fold your hands as if to pray.*
Then Gideon knocked down the place where the people worshiped the false god,	"Ka-blam!"
But he was scared that the people would catch him, so he did it at night. Then God's Spirit filled Gideon and he blew a trumpet	*Make trumpet sounds, "do-do-dado!"*

And many people came to fight against the Midianites.	*Do karate moves!*
And God told him, "You have too many men! Tell anyone who's scared . . .	*Bite your fingernails.*
. . . to go back home!"	"I want my mommy!"
And most of the men ran away!	*Suck your thumb.*
God said, "It's still too many men. Go down to the water to drink and I'll tell you who should stay!"	"Slurp! Slurp! Slurp!"
So Gideon's men went by the water and God told him to send almost all of them away.	"Whoa, Mama!"
Gideon was still a little scared,	*Bite your fingernails*
But God showed him that his army would win!	"That's a relief!"
So then, Gideon told his men that God would save them!	"Hooray!"
Then instead of swords, Gideon gave his men jars and trumpets!	*Make trumpet sounds, "do-do-dado!"*
When Gideon gave the signal, all the men broke their jars	"Ka-plowie!"
And blew their trumpets,	*Make trumpet sounds, "do-do-dado!"*
And yelled really, really loud,	"Ahh!"
And blew their trumpets.	*Make trumpet sounds, "do-do-dado!"*
And they said, "A sword for the Lord and for Gideon!" Let's say that!	"A sword for the Lord and for Gideon!"
The bad guys were so confused they attacked each other!	*Do karate moves!*
God proved he was in charge and that he cared about the safety of his people!	"Hooray!"
The end.	Bow.

Use the following script to have the students form human statues by shaping their bodies into the characters of the story.

It's often helpful to join the children in doing the shaping, or at least to walk around while they're frozen and affirm them for their creative ideas!

Kids, let's become the different people in this story! Pretend your body is a big lump of clay. Now form it into the bad guys! They were mean and took the food from the Israelites and chased them away into caves! 3-2-1 Go! . . . And freeze! . . .

Now, when I count back from three, reshape your body to become like Gideon! Remember, at first he was scared when he thought about being God's leader. Ready? 3-2-1 Go! . . . And freeze! . . .

Now, let's turn into the strong, powerful angel who appeared to Gideon. Ready? 3-2-1 Go! . . . And freeze! Cool!

Now, we'll become the Israelites who were mad when Gideon knocked down the place where they worshiped the false god! They wanted to kill Gideon! 3-2-1 Go! . . . And freeze! . . .

This is going to be a funny one! I want you to make your body like the Israelites when they were sneaking through the woods carrying their trumpets and jars. You need to be sneaky! 3-2-1 Go! . . . And freeze! . . .

OK, when the bad guys heard all those trumpets and the breaking jars, they started fighting each other! So this time, I want you to pull out your weapon—I wonder if it will be a sword or a bow and arrow? Or maybe you know karate! Here we go: 3-2-1 Go! . . . And freeze! . . . Ha! Look at all these bad guys fighting each other!

OK, let's be the Israelites once again, but this time they're not angry or scared, they're brave and happy! Let's see the happy winners in here! They won the fight! 3-2-1 Go! . . . And freeze! . . .

God had rescued them and showed everyone that he was in charge! The end!

End by reviewing how God heard the prayers of his people and chose a special man to be their leader to help them fight the bad guys. Remind the children that when we're afraid or hurting or feel ganged-up-on, God hears our prayers too. Even when we're afraid like Gideon was, God can still use us to do mighty things when we trust in his power rather than ourselves.

Summary

Gideon wasn't super brave,
And he wasn't super strong.
But still he learned to trust in God
When an angel came along.

He learned to lead the people
And they won by breaking jars!
As the Lord scared off those bad guys
Beneath the twinkling stars.

God's people won the battle,
Though their fighting men were few.
And all the people in the land
Learned what the Lord can do.

Chapter 16

Naomi Gets a New Family

BASED ON: Ruth

BIG IDEA: Naomi fostered bitterness against God when she lost her family, but God provided a new family for her and new reasons to be happy.

BACKGROUND: Naomi and her family moved from Bethlehem to another country. There, her husband and sons all died. When she decided to return to her hometown, one of her daughters-in-law insisted on returning with her. Finally she agreed, and she and Ruth moved back to Bethlehem.

However, Naomi was still angry with God and filled with bitterness, telling the women of the town not to call her "Naomi" which means "pleasant," but "Mara" which means "bitter."

But in the end, God worked behind the scenes to provide Naomi with a new family, a family line that would eventually lead to King David, and even to Christ himself.

KEY VERSE: "Then Naomi took the child, laid him in her lap and cared for him. The women living there said, 'Naomi has a son.' And they named him Obed. He was the father of Jesse, the father of David" (Ruth 4:16, 17).

Usually when people tell this story they emphasize Ruth's faithfulness. However, a key to understanding the book of Ruth is to look closely at the life of Naomi. She's the one who struggles the most in this story when she becomes bitter with God. As you tell the story, emphasize how God still loves us even when bad things happen, and that he can grow something happy even out of sad events.

This would be a good time to share a personal story from your life about a time when you were angry with God for some bad (or sad) things that happened, and what you learned in the end about God or about yourself.

For the following story you'll need a cereal box, a lemon, a ring, and a baby's bottle (or pacifier). As you tell the story, you'll hold up the four different items at various times. You can also say the following phrases when you hold up each item:

Baby bottle: **"Goo, goo! Gaa, gaa! Goo, goo! Gaa, gaa!"**
Ring: *(to the tune of "Here Comes the Bride!")* **"Na, na, nana! Na, na, nana!"**
Cereal box: **"I need some food in my tummy, tummy, tummy!"**
Lemon: **"Ew! This is bitter and it's gonna get worse!"**

WHAT TO SAY:	WHAT TO DO:
Long ago there was a woman who had two sons.	Hold up the <u>baby bottle</u>.
One day, she and her husband	Hold up the <u>ring</u>.
Moved away from home because there wasn't much food to eat.	Hold up the <u>cereal box</u>.
After a while the two boys grew up and got married.	Hold up the <u>ring</u>.
But none of them had any babies.	<u>baby bottle</u>
After a while the boys and their father all died. And the woman, whose name was Naomi, thought life had turned bitter and sour.	<u>lemon</u>
She decided to go back to her hometown with Ruth, the wife of one of her sons.	<u>ring</u>
When they arrived, the women said, "Naomi! Is that really you!?" But she told them, "Call me 'Mara' which means bitter, because God has made my life empty and bitter!"	<u>lemon</u>
She and Ruth had little to eat.	Shake the <u>cereal box</u>.

So Ruth went to a farmer's field and the farmer gave her lots of food!	Grin. Pour out some of the <u>cereal</u>.
Naomi could tell the farmer liked Ruth, so she helped them get together and soon they got married!	Happily, hold up the <u>ring</u>.
There was a big party!	Very excitedly, shake all the <u>cereal</u> out of the box.
And it wasn't long before Ruth and her husband had a baby!	<u>baby bottle</u>
And the women stopped calling Naomi "Mara."	<u>lemon</u>
God had filled Naomi's life up again with a new family and new joy. The end.	<u>baby bottle</u>

Explain to the children that Ruth's little baby grew up to become the grandfather of King David, so he was even a relative of Jesus!

Have fun with the following story dramatization:

Ruth went walking in the field to gather some grain. She was hungry. . . . Was it hot? . . . Were there bugs flying all around? . . .

Step over the hole . . .

Climb over the big rock . . .

Jump over the mud puddle. . . . Don't fall in! . . . Oh, no! Wipe off the mud . . .

Look! Some men are getting grain from the field! Ruth isn't here to help them, but she can pick up the grain they drop . . . Pick up some grain . . . Little pieces . . . Big pieces . . . Giant pieces! . . .

And here comes Boaz! He's nice! Look, he's giving us a whole pile of grain! . . . Pick it up! . . . Put it in your pockets! . . . Carry it with both arms! . . . And let's go back to Naomi's house . . . hold it in your arms! . . . Don't drop any grain . . .

Jump over the mud puddle. . . . Oh, no! You dropped some grain. Pick it up! . . .

Climb over the rock . . .

Step over the hole . . .

And OK, we're here! Whew! Drop all the grain on the table! . . . Then Naomi and Ruth baked some bread. . . . Mix it . . . Roll it . . . Pat it . . . Cook it . . . And, mmm! Everybody eat it up! . . .

God took care of Ruth and Naomi and sent them a new friend—Mr. Boaz!

Good job everyone!

Summary

Naomi was angry and she was sad
For her husband and sons had died.
She thought that maybe the Lord was mad
And no longer on her side.

Then Ruth came with her into town
And helped her gather grain.
And Ruth got married to a man
And Boaz was his name.

Soon Ruth was glad to see that she
Had a baby on the way.
And Naomi's life was full again
On that happy exciting day.

Even though Naomi's life
Had often been quite sad,
She got a brand-new family
Which made Naomi glad.

Chapter 17

Samson Battles the Bad Guys

BASED ON: Judges 13–16

BIG IDEA: Samson struggled with wanting to take revenge on people who wronged him, but he was still used by God in a mighty way to fight the enemies of God's people.

BACKGROUND: During the time of the Judges, Israel had no king. The judges served as rulers of the land. One of those judges was a man named Samson, to whom God's Spirit had given superhuman strength. Even though Samson didn't always use wise judgment or honor God with his choices, God still used him in a mighty way to deliver his people. Samson is listed in Hebrews 11:32 as a man of great faith.

KEY VERSE: "Having put him to sleep on her lap, she called a man to shave off the seven braids of his hair, and so began to subdue him. And his strength left him" (Judges 16:19).

While it's true that Samson's battles and exploits are often graphic and violent, he is a great hero of the faith and his stories are important to tell. But that doesn't mean you should focus on the carnage!

Samson struggled with wanting to get even with people, or to get back at them when they did something mean to him. Usually it was his desire for revenge rather than his love for the Lord that prompted him to action. This is one part of the story all of us can relate to and learn from!

The stories about Samson have lots of actions in them so they're easy to act out, but they're also rather violent, so you'll want to use discretion when telling them to younger children.

Here are three different ways to tell this story. Use one, two, or all three ideas to tell and then review the story of God's strong man, Samson.

It's possible to lead the following storymime by yourself, saying and doing all of the parts, but it's usually better to have a partner lead the students in performing the actions while you read or tell the story!

The empty spaces that appear after certain lines are simply there to break up the story and make it easier for you to find and keep your place.

WHAT TO SAY:	WHAT TO DO:
Today's story is about a strong man named Samson!	Flex your muscles.
He was a great warrior . . .	Sword fight.
He was very brave . . .	Put your hands on your hips and stand like Superman.
And he had really long hair . . .	Poof your hair.
AND, a really big secret!	Lean close, finger on your lips.
Here's the secret—God used that long hair	Poof your hair.
to make Samson strong!	Flex your muscles.
Well, one day Samson was walking along the road . . .	Walk in place.
When he saw a lion!	Hand above your eyes, look surprised!
But he didn't run away. Instead, he fought the lion with his bare hands!	Fight the lion.
He might have pushed it over . . .	Push the lion away.
Or even karate chopped it on the head!	Karate chop the lion.
He took care of that lion once and for all!	Wipe your hands against each other.

Another time he had to fight the bad guys, but he wasn't scared!	Put your hands on your hips and stand like Superman.
He used a bone to knock 1000 men over!	Smack the air with your bone.
The bad guys wanted to know what made Samson so strong!	Scratch your head—you're confused!
But he kept it a secret from everyone!	Nod and smile; finger on your lips.
One day, he was with a woman named Delilah. He liked to kiss her on the lips!	Make kissy lips.
But she started working for the bad guys!	Put your hand over your mouth in surprise.
She begged Samson to tell her the secret of his great strength.	Hands together, plead.
And at last he pointed to his nice, long hair . . .	Poof your hair.
That night, he lay down . . .	Make your hands into a pillow.
And went to sleep . . .	Snore.
And while he was asleep, the bad guys snuck in . . .	Tiptoe sneakily.
They shaved off Samson's hair!	Feel for your hair! It's gone!
Now he was weak!	Drop your arms weakly.
They paid Delilah . . .	Weigh some coins in your hand.
And put Samson in jail!	Hold the bars that are next to your face. Look sad.
But he prayed . . .	Fold your hands.
And God gave him great strength once again!	Flex your muscles.
He grabbed the posts of the building . . .	Grab imaginary pillars.
And pulled the whole thing down!	Fall over to the ground.
In the end, Samson had turned to God for help, and that made God happy!	Do a happy dance.
The end.	Take a bow.

Below is a silly way to retell this story using a feather boa as your only prop! You'll want to practice it a few times so you don't have to read the script when you perform it. Also, you'll want to make sure you're familiar with the actions of when and how to manipulate the feather boa.

Once long ago there was a man who was very strong and had long, long hair . . . *(drape the feather boa over your head like long hair, then say, as Samson)* "HUH. COOL!" . . . God is the one who made him so strong, as long as he didn't cut his hair! . . . *(poof your long Samson hair, then say as Samson)* "HUH. COOL!" . . .

He was so strong that when bad guys tried to tie him up . . . *(wrap the boa around your wrists)* he just broke free! *(pull your hands free)*. "HUH. COOL!" . . .

One day, he saw a pretty lady . . . *(drape the boa around your neck and walk like a woman)* . . . She liked Samson and Samson liked her . . . *(drape it back over your head and nod enthusiastically)* "SHE'S COOL!" . . . They wanted to kiss each other on the lips!

But the bad guys . . . *(with one finger, hold the middle of the boa beneath your nose, letting the ends drape down, then do an evil laugh)* "HA! HA! HA!" who had really long mustaches . . . wanted to get Samson!

So, they told that lady . . . *(put it back around your neck)* . . . that if she found out Samson's secret, they'd give her bags of money . . . *(ball up the feather boa, and, holding one end, pretend to weigh it in your hand)*.

So night after night she asked him the secret . . . *(put it back around your neck and pretend to beg)* "PLEASE TELL ME. PLEASE TELL ME. PRETTY, PRETTY, PLEASE!"

Night after night . . . "PLEASE TELL ME. PLEASE TELL ME. PRETTY, PRETTY, PLEASE!" . . . after night, "PLEASE TELL ME. PLEASE TELL ME. PRETTY, PRETTY, PLEASE!"

And finally he told her that the secret was his long hair . . . *(put it back on your head, point to it)* "HUH. COOL!"

So that night when he went to sleep, the bad guys snuck in . . . *(hold it beneath your nose again)* . . . and they shaved off Samson's hair! . . . *(drape it over your head, then yank it off and look surprised)* "UH-OH!" . . . and they paid their helper, that lady named Delilah . . . *(put it back around your neck and act happy and sneaky)* "HEE, HEE, HEE, HEE!"

Then, those bad guys . . . *(hold it beneath your nose again)* . . . took our hero away to the dungeon! But while he was there, his hair began to grow again . . . *(hold it on your head, let the ends drop down)* "HUH. COOL!" . . . and his heart turned back to God. And in the end, Samson pulled down that building on top of all those bad guys . . . *(hold it beneath your nose again)* . . . with the long mustaches . . . *(fall down, then stand up and take a bow)* . . .

The end!

Here's one last way to retell or review the story of Samson using sound effects!

WHAT TO SAY:	WHAT TO SAY:
Samson was a good fighter. He beat up the bad guys!	Karate fighting sounds.
One time, with his bare hands, he fought a lion . . .	Roaring sounds.
And won!	"Poor little kitty!"
One day he fought so hard, he was very, very thirsty . . .	Panting sounds.
Thirstier.	More panting sounds.
Even thirstier!	Lots and lots of panting!
He prayed to God	"Pretty please?"
And God made water come out of the ground	Gurgling sounds
So that Samson would have something to drink.	"Ah!"
Usually, he tried to get back at the bad guys if they hurt him!	Karate fighting sounds.
He met a pretty lady.	"Ooh-la-la!"
And when he was sleeping . . .	Snoring sounds.
She told the bad guys to cut off his hair!	"Snip! Snip!"
And he was bald!	"Uh-oh!"
And sad.	"Waa!"
And weak!	"Uh-oh."
They stuck him in the dungeon, where there were rats!	Make nibbling gnawing sounds.
But there, he prayed to God!	"Please help me!"
Then he pulled down the building!	Crashing sounds.
On top of all the bad guys!	"Uh-oh!"
God used Samson to battle the enemies of the land!	"Hooray!"
The end.	Take a bow.

Summary

Oh, Samson was so very brave
And he was very strong.
His muscles were so very big
And his hair was very long.
He fought Philistines with a bone!
And a lion with his hands!
'Til he told her, "It's my hair!"
So the bad guys came and shaved his head
And he was bald up there.

They stuck him in a dungeon
And Samson said a prayer.
And God began to give him strength
And help him grow his hair.
Then Samson pulled the building down,
And the bad guys were no more.
Yes, Samson had great strength,
As Samson served the Lord.

Chapter 18

Samuel Meets the Lord

BASED ON: 1 Samuel 3

BIG IDEA: Samuel learned to listen to God's voice and share what God had to say. He became one of God's greatest spokespersons.

BACKGROUND: Samuel was the long-awaited son of a prayerful woman named Hannah. Since she had promised to dedicate him to the Lord, she took him to the worship place while he was still a young boy, and he began to live there. Samuel helped the aging priest Eli with the chores since his eyesight was failing.

   God had warned Eli that he should do a better job of disciplining his sons or there would be severe consequences (1 Samuel 2:27-36). Then one night, God spoke to Samuel. Though at first he was confused about who was talking to him, young Samuel listened. The next morning he delivered God's word to Eli, even though he knew it was news Eli wouldn't want to hear. Consequently, Samuel became one of God's most trusted and faithful prophets.

KEY VERSE: "The LORD was with Samuel as he grew up, and he let none of his words fall to the ground" (1 Samuel 3:19).

Just like so many Bible stories, this story has a series of events that happened three times. Once you start to look for this pattern in the stories you tell, it'll be easier to learn and remember them. Typically, when events happen three times, the "third time is the charm." That's the way it is in this story. The third time Samuel went to Eli, Eli realized that the voice in the night must be God speaking to Samuel.

Also, this story is a good example of the transformation of a situation and a person. At the beginning of the story, Israel had no prophet speaking for the Lord and Samuel did not yet know the Lord. At the end of the story, both situations are reversed.

Since this story happens in the temple at night, you may wish to turn off the classroom lights and place a few lighted candles around the room. (Make sure they're not in places where the children will knock them over while you're doing the activities related to the story!)

Samuel had a special job. He was the one at the temple of God who had to . . . *(pull out a candle)* **. . . light the candles and . . .** *(pull out a broom or a dustpan)* **. . . sweep the floor and . . .** *(a feather duster)* **. . . clean the corners of the room.**

One night he was . . . *(a teddy bear)* **. . . sleeping. Suddenly he heard someone call . . .** *(cell phone)* **. . . no, it wasn't someone on a cell phone! But it was someone calling his name. He thought it was Eli, the priest. So he . . .** *(running shoe)* **. . . ran to Eli, but Eli shook his head. "It wasn't me," said Eli.**

This happened three times. Samuel . . . *(a teddy bear)* **. . . went back to sleep. He heard . . .** *(cell phone)* **. . . someone call his name. And he . . .** *(running shoe)* **. . . ran to Eli. Finally, Eli realized it was God calling, and he told Samuel to say yes to God!** *(look up toward the sky to talk to God)* **"Is that you, God? I'll listen and do whatever you say!"**

But the next day he went back to his jobs. He started to . . . *(pull out a candle)* **. . . light the candles and . . .** *(pull out a broom or a dustpan)* **. . . sweep the floor and . . .** *(a feather duster)* **. . . clean the corners of the room. Until Eli asked him what God had said.**

So . . . *(Bible)* **. . . Samuel told Eli God's Word. And from then on, Samuel became the person who told the people in the land what God had to say. The end!**

Here's a version of the story that includes lots of actions for the children. Your students will enjoy the repetition of events because they'll be able to look forward to their part in the story.

For this story, I'm going to be the storyteller, and *(insert the name of another leader or one of the students whom you have chosen)* is going to be Eli. And you *(the class)* are going to be Samuel! Eli starts the story over there, on the other side of the room.

The people of Israel were sad because they didn't have anyone to tell them God's messages. Show me how sad they were! . . .

Samuel was a boy who helped clean the worship place. . . . Well, one night Samuel was asleep. Can you pretend to be asleep? . . . And then God spoke to him, "Samuel! Samuel!" But Samuel didn't know it was God talking.

Samuel woke up . . . sat up . . . stood up . . . and ran to Eli! Everybody run to Eli! . . . And Samuel said, "I came right away when I heard what you said!" Let's say that with Samuel: "I CAME RIGHT AWAY WHEN I HEARD WHAT YOU SAID!"

But Eli told him, "It wasn't me calling you; go back to bed!" *(Encourage the person playing Eli to say those words.)*

OK, everyone! Come on back to bed! . . . Then, Samuel lay down . . . closed his eyes . . . and went to sleep . . . He might have even snored . . . But once again God spoke to him: "Samuel! Samuel!" Samuel woke up . . . sat up . . . stood up . . . and ran to Eli! Everybody run to Eli! . . . And he said, "I came right away when I heard what you said!" Ready? "I CAME RIGHT AWAY WHEN I HEARD WHAT YOU SAID!"

But Eli told him, "It wasn't me calling you; go back to bed!" *(Encourage the person playing Eli to say those words.)*

So, he went back to bed! . . . Then, he lay down . . . closed his eyes . . . and went to sleep . . . I'll bet he snored a lot this time . . . For the third time that night God spoke to him: "Samuel! Samuel!" And for the third time that night, Samuel didn't know it was God!

So he woke up . . . sat up . . . rubbed his eyes . . . yawned . . . stood up . . . and ran to Eli! Everybody run to Eli! . . . Run faster, you're in a hurry! . . . And he said, "I came right away when I heard what you said!" Ready? "I CAME RIGHT AWAY WHEN I HEARD WHAT YOU SAID!"

But this time Eli realized it was God calling out to Samuel. He told Samuel, "Tell God, 'I'm here and I'm listening!'" *(Encourage the person playing Eli to say those words.)*

So, Samuel went back to bed! . . . Then, he lay down . . . closed his eyes . . . and went to sleep . . . snoring loudly . . . And once again, God spoke to him: "Samuel! Samuel!" And this time when he woke up, he sat up . . . stood up . . . and said, "I'm here and I'm listening and I'm ready to serve!" Let's say that. Ready? "I'M HERE AND I'M LISTENING AND I'M READY TO SERVE!"

And God told Samuel to tell Eli a very important message. So then, Samuel tried to go back to sleep . . . But I don't think he slept too much . . . I think he probably rolled back and forth a lot . . .

In the morning, he sat up . . . stood up . . . and DIDN'T run to Eli! He started doing all his other work first, like sweeping the floor . . . turning on the lights . . . feeding the iguana—OK, he didn't feed the iguana, but he did wait for Eli and finally, Eli came to him and asked him what the Lord had said.

At first, Samuel didn't want to tell him *(Shake your head, "no")* . . . but then at last he told Eli the message from God. *(Nod)* . . . And from then on, Samuel told the people all over the land all the messages God told him. *(Two thumbs up)* . . . And he was famous from one end of the country to the other.

The end!

Summary

In the middle of a night,
Both dark and deep.
A boy named Samuel
Lay fast asleep.
Then he heard a voice
Ring loud and clear.
It was calling his name
From someplace near!
So Samuel ran
To Eli's bed.
But he hadn't been calling
He was sleeping instead!

So back to his bed
The little boy ran
And once again
He heard a man
Calling his name
In the middle
Of the night
And he thought it was Eli
But he wasn't right!

At last Eli said,
"It's really God's voice!"
Then Samuel listened
And he made a choice.
He would speak for God
And make a new start.
And he followed the Lord
With all of his heart!

Chapter 19

Saul Discovers He'll Be the King

BASED ON: 1 Samuel 9, 10

BIG IDEA: God chose Saul to be the king of the land and announced this decision through the prophet Samuel.

BACKGROUND: Samuel had been Israel's leader for a long time. He appointed his sons to be leaders, but they were corrupt and greedy. So God's people asked him to appoint a king to rule over them. Samuel prayed about it, and God revealed to him that this choice was their way of rejecting the Lord as their ruler.

Samuel warned the people about how a king would exact taxes and call their sons and daughters into service, but the people didn't care. In the end, God told Samuel to anoint a king over the land.

Today's story is the account of how Saul discovered that God had chosen him to be the king.

KEY VERSE: "Then Samuel took a flask of oil and poured it on Saul's head and kissed him, saying, 'Has not the LORD anointed you leader over his inheritance?'" (1 Samuel 10:1).

Israel wanted to be like the other nations. Rather than letting the Lord be their king, they wanted a human king that they could see. Finally, God gave in to their demands and he sent his prophet Samuel to anoint Saul as the first king of Israel.

In a humorous display of his sovereignty, God used a bunch of lost donkeys to introduce Saul to Samuel!

Your imaginary search for the donkeys will be somewhat different from the one printed below since it will depend on the suggestions of your students. As you lead the activity, act out the gestures with the students.

Be aware that when you say something like, "Don't fall off the mountain!" Many of the children (usually the boys!) will immediately do it. That's OK. Play off it and accept it. Say something like, "No, *don't* fall off the mountain!" at which time, the rest of the class will do it! This is just the students being playful; it isn't willful disobedience. Help them to understand by your response that there are times to be silly and times to be serious, and this is one time when it's OK to be playful and have fun.

> **Saul's dad sent him on a search. It was a very important job. He had to find his father's lost donkeys! Let's pretend we're looking for those lost donkeys! Where should we look?** . . . *(Accept whatever suggestions the students offer. Listed below are examples of what might be said.)* **. . . OK! Let's look on the mountain. Everyone, climb the mountain . . .** *(act like a rock climber)* **. . . Don't fall! . . . OK, let's climb over the top of the mountain . . . Nope. No donkeys. Where else can we look? . . .**
>
> **Great! Let's look in a cave . . . Everyone pull out your flashlight . . . Duck down! . . . Don't hit your head on the ceiling! . . . Sneak through the cave . . . And—oh, no! Bats! . . . Run out of the cave! . . .**
>
> **Hmm . . . where else should we look? . . . OK, let's look by the river! Let's all wade into the river . . . And, oh, no! It's too deep! . . . Swim! . . . Swim through the river! . . .** *(climbing out of the river)* **. . . Whew! We made it to the other side!**
>
> **OK, let's look in one more place for the donkeys. Where do you think Saul looked for his dad's donkeys? . . . Um, Wal-Mart?! OK, why not . . .** *(grab your shopping cart)* **. . . OK,**

let's see . . . There are the hamburgers . . . And the candy bars . . . And the . . . DONKEYS! Whoa! Stick the donkeys in your shopping cart . . . And let's go home to celebrate! Yea!

Whatever the children suggest, at the end of your imaginary search, find the donkeys. Then transition to the Bible story by saying something like this: **"Actually, the donkeys were found in the Bible story, but not by Saul. (And not at Wal-Mart!) Instead, Saul found something else that was even more valuable than the donkeys! Listen to the rest of the story to find out what it was!"**

After saying the short refrains in the following story, pause long enough to let the children repeat them. Practice the story a couple times before performing it in front of the class.

> **After Saul couldn't find the donkeys** *(hee haw! hee haw)*, **he was ready to go back home so his dad wouldn't worry about him** *(oh, dear! where is that boy?)*. **But instead, his friend suggested they ask one of God's teachers for help** *(hmm . . . that's a good idea!)*. **The teacher they talked to was named Samuel.**
>
> **Now, God had told Samuel that the donkeys** *(hee haw! hee haw)* **had been found. And God had also told Samuel that Saul would be the king of the land!** *(hip, hip hooray!)* **So when Saul came to visit, Samuel had a big dinner in his honor** *(yum! yum!)*, **and then Samuel told him, "The Lord has made you the king of the land!"** *(long live the king!)*
>
> **Saul could hardly believe it! But to prove this was from God, Samuel told Saul that on his trip back home, he would meet three groups of people** *(uno, dos, tres)*. **"The first will ask about the donkeys** *(hee haw! hee haw!)*, **the second will offer you a meal,** *(yum! yum!)* **and when you meet the third group, God's Spirit will fill you up and you'll tell people the words of God!"** *(hallelujah, praise the Lord!)*
>
> **When Saul left, everything happened just as Samuel had said! The first group asked about the donkeys . . .** *(hee haw! hee haw!)*, **the second group offered him a meal** *(yum! yum!)* **and when he met the third group, God's Spirit filled him up and he told people the words of God!** *(hallelujah, praise the Lord!)*
>
> **Meanwhile someone else found the donkeys** *(hee haw! hee haw!)*, **but Saul found something even better. He discovered God's plan for his life** *(long live the king!)*. **And he found out just how important he was to God** *(hip, hip hooray!)*. **And God's Spirit came into his heart** *(hallelujah, praise the Lord!)*.
>
> **The end.**

When you're done you may wish to review that God chose Saul to be the leader, God's Spirit filled his heart, and Saul discovered God's exciting plan for his life.

This would be a good chance to tell a personal story from your life about a time when you (1) found out you'd been chosen for something important, (2) God changed your heart and filled you with his Spirit, or (3) you discovered God's plan for your life.

You can remind the students that God also chooses us to be his children; he also changes our hearts when we trust in him; and he also has an exciting plan for each one of us. End with a prayer of thanks to God for all the wonderful and exciting things he has planned for each of us!

The Bible tells us to pray for our leaders. Remind the children that, just like Samuel or Saul, our leaders today need God's help and wisdom. You might wish to pray this prayer with the children:

> *God, bless all our leaders in all that they do*
> *Give 'em honor and boldness and wisdom from you.*
> *All our governors, soldiers, policemen, and chiefs,*
> *Who work for our country and protect our beliefs.*
> *And the congressmen, senators, judges, and spies,*
> *Make 'em smart! Make 'em noble!*
> *Courageous and wise!*
> *Help 'em fight for more justice and do what is right.*
> *God, please bless our leaders today and tonight.*
> *Amen.*

Summary

Saul went on a donkey hunt
To see what he could find.
He met a man named Samuel
They ate
     And drank
          And dined.

Then Sam said Saul would be the king,
And he would be his friend.
Yes, Israel's king was found the day
The hunt came to an end!

Chapter 20

David Fights the Giant

BASED ON: 1 Samuel 17:1-52

BIG IDEA: David trusted in God for victory when he went to fight Goliath. God still gives victory to people who trust in him when they face giant-sized problems in their lives.

BACKGROUND: The Israelites were once again facing their dreaded enemies, the Philistines. The only problem was, no one in the Israelite army (including King Saul) was brave enough to fight against the Philistine champion Goliath. Then David, a young shepherd, stepped up to the challenge armed only with a slingshot, a shepherd's staff, and an unyielding faith in God. Through David, God delivered his people from the Philistines and gave them the victory.

KEY VERSE: "So David triumphed over the Philistine with a sling and a stone; without a sword in his hand he struck down the Philistine and killed him" (1 Samuel 17:50).

Today's story is one of the most famous stories in the whole Bible. And, once again (as with many Old Testament stories), this story has more graphic violence than is appropriate for most young children. For example, you'll probably want to leave out the part about David slicing off Goliath's head after he knocked him down!

The following sound effects story is easy to lead, and fun for the children. Practice it a couple of times to learn the rhythm of the sound effects. Also, tell the children that you'll be saying each sound one time through, and then they'll join you two more times. You'll want to make sure they understand that they don't just keep saying the refrains over and over and over again.

WHAT TO SAY:	SOUNDS TO MAKE:
David had to watch the sheep.	Baa. Baa. Baa-y baa. Baa. Baa. Baa-y baa. Baa. Baa. Baa-y baa.
One day, his dad sent him to take food to his brothers	Yum. Yum. Yummy yum. Yum. Yum. Yummy yum. Yum. Yum. Yummy yum.
who were at the war.	Fight. Fight. Fighty fight. Fight. Fight. Fighty fight. Fight. Fight. Fighty fight.
To get there, sometimes he had to walk through the tall grass.	Swish. Swish. Swishy swish. Swish. Swish. Swishy swish. Swish. Swish. Swishy swish.
And sometimes he had to walk through the mud!	Squish. Squish. Squishy squish. Squish. Squish. Squishy squish. Squish. Squish. Squishy squish.
When he arrived at the war, he saw that his friends and family were scared!	Shake. Shake. Shaky shake. Shake. Shake. Shaky shake. Shake. Shake. Shaky shake.
Because the other side had a giant!	Stomp. Stomp. Stompy stomp. Stomp. Stomp. Stompy stomp. Stomp. Stomp. Stompy stomp.

But David trusted in God! He wasn't scared! So he went down by the stream.	Gurgle. Gurgle. Gurgly gurgle. Gurgle. Gurgle. Gurgly gurgle. Gurgle. Gurgle. Gurgly gurgle.
He grabbed some stones, and then ran toward the giant!	Sprint. Sprint. Sprinty sprint! Sprint. Sprint. Sprinty sprint! Sprint. Sprint. Sprinty sprint!
He put a rock in his slingshot and sent the rock flying toward the giant!	Whoosh. Whoosh. Whooshy whoosh! Whoosh. Whoosh. Whooshy whoosh! Whoosh. Whoosh. Whooshy whoosh!
It hit him on the head!	Ow. Ow. Owie ow. Ow. Ow. Owie ow. Ow. Ow. Owie ow.
The giant fell to the ground!	Thump. Thump. Thumpy thump. Thump. Thump. Thumpy thump. Thump. Thump. Thumpy thump.
And all the men in the giant's army ran away, scared!	Yikes! Yikes! Yikey Yikes! Yikes! Yikes! Yikey Yikes! Yikes! Yikes! Yikey Yikes!
David and his friends won the battle because David had trusted in God!	Hip. Hip. Hip hooray! Hip. Hip. Hip hooray! Hip. Hip. Hip hooray!
The end.	Done. Done. Doney done! Done. Done. Doney done! Done. Done. Doney done!

Here's a way to act out the story together. Pause whenever the ellipses appear to allow the students (and you) enough time to do the actions.

Long ago, the people of Israel were lined up for battle. Some had swords. Show me your swords! . . . Some had a bow and arrow . . . Others had slingshots . . . None of them had fighter jets . . . No, none of them were flying around in fighter jets! . . .

Their enemies were ready to fight them. The Philistines had swords . . . and bows . . . and slingshots . . . and one extra special weapon—no it wasn't a fighter jet . . . they had a giant! Show me how big that giant was! . . . His name was Goliath and he stomped out to talk to the Israelites. Stomp like a giant! . . . Good! . . . Stomp . . . Stomp . . . Stomp . . .

"Fight me!" he yelled. Go ahead and yell like a giant, ready? "FIGHT ME!"

But the Israelites were so scared they stood there shaking . . . Show me how scared they were! . . . Did their knees shake? . . . Did they bite their fingernails? . . . Did they cry out for their mommies? . . .

Now, David was in charge of protecting the sheep. What do you think those sheep sounded like? . . . But David was very brave. Stand up tall with your hands on your hips like Superman . . .

Well, David walked to the battlefield . . . He thought he would see a big fight going on, but instead he found the Israelites shaking and scared . . . and crying out for their mommies . . .

"I'll fight the giant!" he said. Go ahead and say it like brave Dave: "I'LL FIGHT THE GIANT!" . . . And then he said, "I believe in God!" Let's say that: "I BELIEVE IN GOD!"

Then Dave picked up some rocks . . . Um, they were little rocks, not big boulders! . . . I said he <u>didn't</u> pick up any big boulders . . . Oh well . . . And he ran toward the giant. Show me how fast he ran . . . Wow! . . . And he used his slingshot and sent the rock flying at the giant! Go ahead! . . . Um, David did not use a fighter jet to attack the giant . . .

OK, pretend to be the giant again. The rock hits you in the head! . . . and knocks you over . . . you're hurt really bad . . . Good acting!

Then, all the Philistines ran away yelling . . . and the Israelites won the battle and were so happy! . . . David was a hero and all the people cheered for God. Go ahead, let me hear you cheer for God! . . .

The end.

Finally, here's a chant you can use to review the story! Repeat it as desired and get faster and faster each time through!

Sheep! *(make sheep ears)*
Creek! *(wiggle fingers to represent water)*
Giant! *(stand tall like a giant)*
Roar! *(make mean faces)*

(Repeat this three times.)

David knocked him down! *(flop your arms down)*
And he was no more! *(shake your head and your arms back and forth)*

Summary

David went to fight the giant
Walking all alone
He took along a slingshot
      And a shiny little stone.
The giant laughed;
He thought that David
Couldn't win the fight.
But David really loved the Lord
And trusted in his might.

Then David ran straight toward Goliath
To do what he said he'd do.
His rock went flying through the air
And Goliath's days were through!
For David's faith was super strong
So what more can I say?
The giant fell and the people knew
That God had saved the day!

Chapter 21

David and Jonathan Become Friends

BASED ON: 1 Samuel 18–20

BIG IDEA: Jonathan and David were close friends. They cared about each other and loved God. Their love for God was a big part of their strong and enduring friendship.

BACKGROUND: After David's victory over Goliath, King Saul became jealous of David's popularity. Saul's son, Jonathan, became close friends with David, and this angered Saul even more.

   Saul repeatedly tried to kill David, but failed. This only served to inflame Saul's hatred toward David!

   In this story, Jonathan and David promised that they would remain friends with each other forever, no matter what.

KEY VERSE: "Jonathan said to David, 'Go in peace, for we have sworn friendship with each other in the name of the LORD'" (1 Samuel 20:42).

If you talk about how Jonathan and David kissed each other goodbye (see 1 Samuel 20:41), be sure the children understand that in those days people didn't shake hands or give hugs so much, but kissed people on the cheek as a way of saying hello or goodbye. (You don't want your students to think there was anything inappropriate about the friendship of these two men.)

We can learn from Jonathan and David's friendship to respect and stand up for our friends. This story shows what a strong friendship David and Jonathan had. It gives you a good chance to talk about caring for your friends!

The following story includes ideas for both actions and props. Use whichever (or both) as desired when you tell the story.

WHAT TO SAY:	SUGGESTED ACTIONS:	SUGGESTED PROPS:
Saul was angry.	Make fists and an angry face!	A crown.
He knew David was famous and brave and he wanted to be just as famous and brave.	Stand tall and brave!	
Now, in those days, Saul was the king.	Set a crown on your head.	
David played the harp for him.	Play your harps!	Strum a guitar.
But Saul was so mad, he threw a spear at David!	Throw your spears.	Throw a straw at the students.
It missed David and he kept playing the harp.	Play your harps again.	Strum the guitar again.
Then Saul threw the spear again!	Throw your spears!	Throw another straw.
So David left and Jonathan, the king's son, asked him if he was going to have supper with them.	Eat lots of food!	A fork.
"Your dad keeps throwing spears at me!" said David.	Throw your spears!	Throw a straw at the children.
Well, Jonathan could hardly believe it.	Look shocked.	A fork.
He told David he'd find out if it was really true	Tap to your chest.	
Then Jonathan went to supper.	Eat lots of food!	

David and Jonathan Become Friends 69

His dad was so mad at him for being David's friend that he threw a spear at Jonathan!	Throw your spears!	Throw a straw at the children.
So Jonathan left to warn David in the field.	Walk in place.	A handful of grass.
He was sad because he knew his dad might kill him for being friends with David,	Cry.	Throw a straw.
but no matter what, he wasn't going to stop caring about his harp-playing friend David.	Smile. Show resolve.	Play the guitar.
The end.		

Explain that when Jonathan pledged his friendship to David at the end of the story, he was saying, "Even if my dad tries to kill you, I'll always be your friend." That's a great model of friendship! According to Jesus, there's no greater love than the willingness to lay down your life for a friend (John 15:13).

As you read (or tell) the following dramatized story, be sure to pause long enough for the students to do the actions wherever the ellipses appear.

OK kids, everyone stand up! You're going to help me tell this story in a special way!

One day David woke up early. He yawned . . . and stretched his arms . . . and then hurried out to the field! . . . Then he hid behind a great big rock. Find a rock and hide behind it, quick, before anyone comes! . . . Good hiding! Where did everybody go? I can't see you!

Now, pretty soon Jonathan came to the field. OK kids, you can stop hiding. Now, you need to pretend to be Jonathan, David's friend. He was strong and brave . . . Jonathan was walking to the field . . . Carrying his bow and arrow . . . Do you have a small bow or a big one? . . . Wow! There are some really big bows in here!

Jonathan put an arrow in his bow . . . he drew back the bow . . . and he shot the arrow as far as he could! . . . No, he did not shoot the arrow at the teacher! . . . I said he DIDN'T! . . . Oh, brother.

Then, the boy who was helping Jonathan ran to get the arrow . . . OK kids, go and get your arrows! I don't know where they are . . . Some are stuck in the wall over there! . . . Where is your arrow? . . . Everyone find your arrows! . . .

When Jonathan told the boy to go farther and get the arrows, it was a special clue for David to know he needed to run far away because Saul really did want to hurt him!

So the boy brought the arrow back to Jonathan . . . Bring your arrows back here, everyone . . . Carry them carefully; don't poke yourself in the foot . . .

Then the boy took the bow and the arrows and went back to town . . . Goodbye boy! . . .

And David and Jonathan met. Shake hands with someone . . . Or maybe give 'em a hug . . . Actually David and Jonathan didn't hug or shake hands; they kissed each other on the cheek! But you don't have to do that today . . .

They were happy to see each other . . . but sad because David had to go far away for a long time . . . So they cried . . . They cried really loudly! . . . But David cried the most! . . .

And they told each other, "We're friends forever, and friends with God!" Let's say that together: "WE'RE FRIENDS FOREVER, AND FRIENDS WITH GOD!"

Then they waved goodbye to each other . . . and went home.

The end.

Summary

Saul was very angry
So he grabbed a sharp spear
And threw it through the air
At David's left ear!

But he missed him twice
And that was good.
Because Saul wasn't acting
The way that he should.

Now Jonathan and David
Were super good friends.
They had the kind of friendship
That never, ever ends.

But Jon couldn't believe
What his dad had just done
'Til Saul threw a spear
At his very own son!

Still Jonathan and David
Were not afraid to say
That they'd always be best friends,
Whatever came their way.

Chapter 22

David Dances Before the Lord

BASED ON: 2 Samuel 6:12-23

BIG IDEA: David was not ashamed of expressing his joy and thanksgiving by dancing wholeheartedly to the Lord.

BACKGROUND: The Ark of the Covenant hadn't been in the city of Jerusalem for quite some time. David went to retrieve it, but became angry with God (and afraid) because God punished a man who treated the ark irreverently.

But in time, David heard that God was blessing a different man who was watching over the ark, so he went once again to get it and return it to Jerusalem. He knew God wasn't angry at him and he celebrated all the way back, leading the people in worship and praise to the Lord.

KEY VERSE: "David, wearing a linen ephod, danced before the LORD with all his might, while he and the entire house of Israel brought up the ark of the LORD with shouts and the sound of trumpets" (2 Samuel 6:14, 15).

When you read this story in the Bible, you'll read about how Uzzah died when he treated the Ark of the Covenant irreverently (earlier in 2 Samuel 6). This was an expression of how holy God is. You don't need to discuss this aspect of the story with the children. Instead, contrast King David and Queen Michal's responses: David cared only about what God thought; Michal cared only about what other people thought.

First, tell this story to the children, and then have fun acting (and dancing) it out!

> Long ago, King David wanted to bring a special box back to the city. The box held things that were important to God!
>
> But the box had to be treated in a very special way and David was afraid God might be angry if he didn't treat it right. But when David heard that the man watching the box was happy, he knew God wasn't mad. So David went to go get it. As the men carried the box back to the city, David showed how happy and thankful he was by dancing with all his might!
>
> But when his wife saw that, she thought he was being silly and thought people might not listen to him anymore. But King David said, "I'll dance even more than this to show how much I love the Lord!"
>
> And God was very happy with David's dance.
>
> The end.
>
> OK! Let's learn a little song and do our own dance for God!

Young children love to jump around. This story will give you a great chance to let them get their wiggles out! You may even want to play some exciting music while you dance to the Lord!

> **Once there was a king and his name was Dave,** *(Put on your crowns!)*
> **His name was Dave,** *(Repeat.)*
> **His name was Dave.** *(Repeat.)*
> **Once there was a king and his name was Dave,** *(Etc…)*
> **And he danced before the Lord!** *(Dance wild and weird for God!)*

He jumped up and down with all his might, *(Jump around!)*
All his might, *(Etc…)*
All his might.
He jumped up and down with all his might,
As he danced before the Lord! *(Dance for the Lord again!)*

His wife wasn't happy when she saw what he did, *(Hands on your hips, be angry!)*
Saw what he did,
Saw what he did.
His wife wasn't happy when she saw what he did,
When he danced before the Lord! *(Dance!)*

She said, "It is silly when you act this way, *(Scold with your finger!)*
Act this way,
Act this way.
She said, "It is silly when you act this way,
And you dance before the Lord!" *(Dance!)*

But David told her he was gonna dance even more! *(Dance crazy with your arms!)*
Dance even more!
Dance even more!
But David told her he was gonna dance even more,
As he danced before the Lord! *(Dance!)*

So whenever you are happy and you want to dance, *(Huge smiles, dance a little!)*
You want to dance.
You want to dance.
Whenever you are happy and you want to dance,
Go and dance before the Lord! *(Dance a lot to God!)*

Consider handing out ribbons or streamers to help create a more colorful, lively dance. Then, explore different ways of dancing or moving for the Lord!

Every time we move it can be for God, in everything we do!
Let's explore different ways that we can dance or move for the Lord!
Let's gallop for God! Ready? Go! . . .
Gallop for God!
Gallop for God!
Gallop for God today!
(Repeat)

Good! Good galloping! Now, let's do a tiptoe dance! Ready? Go! . . .
Tiptoe for God!
Tiptoe for God!
Tiptoe for God today!
(Repeat)

Great! Let's do a fast dance for God . . .
Fast dance for God!
Fast dance for God!

Fast dance for God today!
(Repeat)

And a slow dance . . .
What other ways can we dance for God today?

Explore different types of movement. For example: bending, crawling, floating, hopping, leaping, marching, rolling, shaking, shrinking, skipping, slinking, slithering, soaring, spinning, stomping, stretching, swaying, swinging, twisting. (Um, you probably won't do every idea on this list!)

Summary

David was so happy
That he did a little dance!
    David jumped
    And David sang
    And David clapped his hands!

He didn't really care
What the other people said.
But his wife was so upset
That she sighed and shook her head.
    "David, you're the king
    And you're acting really wild!
    You should act more like a grown-up
    And not a little child!"
But David only said
As he twirled and swirled around,
    "My dear, I'll dance even more than this
    As I travel through the town!"

Well, God was very happy
With David's dancing ways
For he loves it
    When we worship him
        And offer him our praise.

Chapter 23

Solomon Searches for Happiness

BASED ON:	Ecclesiastes 1–5
BIG IDEA:	Nothing apart from God can provide true happiness and meaning in life.
BACKGROUND:	King Solomon (the son of King David), tried to find happiness many different ways in his life. During his search he found that without God at the center of life, pleasure, wisdom, foolishness, hard work, injustice and job promotion are all meaningless.
KEY VERSE:	"When God gives any man wealth and possessions, and enables him to enjoy them, to accept his lot and be happy in his work—this is a gift of God" (Ecclesiastes 5:19).

Young children can understand that everyone wants to be happy. They do too! When you introduce this story, you could ask them to talk about the things that make them unhappy. If you invite them to tell you about the things that make them happy, you'd be focusing on the solution and not the struggle. Remember, good stories are about struggles. That's what makes them interesting! You could introduce the story by saying, "Today's story is about a man who wanted very much to be happy. Let's find out if he discovered a way to be happy deep in his heart." Then in closing say something like this: "Many things in life can make us unhappy. Only God's love can make our hearts truly and deeply happy forever."

Solomon was a very rich man. He wanted to be happy so he decided to build nice houses! Let's pretend to build a house, OK? Saw the wood . . . hammer it . . . pour the concrete. . . . What do you think he put in those nice big houses? . . . What else? . . . But even with all that nice stuff, he was still unhappy!
Because when you don't follow the Lord from the start,
HOUSES will not make you happy deep inside your heart.

So he decided to eat anything he wanted to in the whole wide world to try and be happy! What do you think Solomon ate? . . . Yup! What else? . . . Yes! Go ahead and eat a great big juicy one! . . . But he was still unhappy!
Because when you don't follow the Lord from the start,
SNACKS will not make you happy deep inside your heart.

He learned many things reading books, . . . *(pretend to read a book)* building great big palaces, . . . *(build)* . . . and planting pretty gardens. . . . *(plant)* . . . But he was still unhappy!
Because when you don't follow the Lord from the start,
BOOKS will not make you happy deep inside your heart.
PALACES won't make you happy deep inside your heart.
GARDENS will not make you happy deep inside your heart.

So then Solomon started to go to parties! What's your favorite thing to do at a party? . . . Do you think Solomon did that? . . . Do you think it made him happy deep inside his heart? . . . Sometimes he tried to be happy by laughing more. Let's laugh like Solomon . . . Now laugh lots and lots like Solomon! . . . Good! And sometimes he just plain acted stupid *(or "foolish")*. Can you act stupid *(or "foolish")*? . . . My, that's very good! But he was still unhappy!

Because when you don't follow the Lord from the start,
PARTIES will not make you happy deep inside your heart.
ACTING STUPID (or "foolish") will not make you happy deep inside your heart.

He dug holes so water would go to the fields and help the plants grow. Let's dig . . . Bigger holes! . . . Don't fall in! . . .

He planted all kinds of fruit trees . . . *(pick some fruit, take a bite)* . . . And he bought lots of cows, sheep, and chickens! Do you think it was noisy? . . . What did the cows sound like? . . . The sheep? . . . The chickens? . . . But he was still unhappy!

Because when you don't follow the Lord from the start,
FRUIT will not make you happy deep inside your heart.
ANIMALS won't make you happy deep inside your heart.

Finally, he thought, "Hmm . . . a lot of these things are good and come from God. But if we don't do them because we love God, they won't make us happy at all. Nothing can make us happy forever except following God!"

But when you DO follow the Lord from the start,
All of life can make you happy deep inside your heart!

You could also tell this story with props in a story bag. Collect toys, stuffed animals, and books, as well as some silly or unexpected objects (such as a rubber chicken, or duct tape). Place all of the objects in a large bag or box. Pull them out as you tell the story and ask the children if they think that object can make them happy deep inside their hearts. The children will pay attention because they'll be curious about what you're going to pull out next!

Summary

Solomon the king searched for happiness and fun
But everything he tried left him sad when he was done.
    He planted gardens in the shade
    And flowers in the sun,
But everything he tried left him sad when he was done!

Building palaces and houses, planting fields full of grain.
    Digging tunnels underground
    To funnel in the rain.
Buying cows and sheep and chickens and
Protecting every one
But everything he tried left him sad when he was done.

Solomon read books and went to parties every night!
    He listened to the singers
    Sing their songs and do it right.
He ate big meals and sometimes he ate more than anyone!
But everything he tried left him sad when he was done.

Finally he learned a secret—that happiness won't come
From being either rich or poor
Or even smart or dumb!
'Cause every single day
That we live beneath the sun,
Happiness can only come
When God is number one!

Chapter 24

God Provides for Elijah

BASED ON:	1 Kings 17
BIG IDEA:	God provided for Elijah the prophet in a miraculous way during a drought.
BACKGROUND:	Ahab and his family were wicked rulers in the northern kingdom (Israel). As a result, God's prophet Elijah prayed that God would not send rain or dew on the land.
	The drought lasted for three years and during that time God provided for Elijah in two miraculous ways. First, by having ravens bring him food while he lived in the wilderness near a brook. Later, after the brook dried up, God continued to care for him by miraculously refilling the flour and cooking oil of a widow with whom Elijah went to stay.
KEY VERSE:	"This is what the LORD, the God of Israel, says: 'The jar of flour will not be used up and the jug of oil will not run dry until the day the LORD gives rain on the land'" (1 Kings 17:14).

Many of the Israelites were worshiping false gods, following the example of the wicked King Ahab. During that time, God told Elijah to pray that it wouldn't rain, and that's what he did. For more than three years there was a drought in the land. God used this as a way to wake his people up to how useless the false gods were and how important it was to worship the one true God.

Elijah was one of the Lord's greatest prophets. He had many adventures. Today's lesson covers the different ways that God provided for him in the years leading up to his famous showdown with the prophets of Baal on Mount Carmel. Because of the violent nature of that story, we'll leave that for older students and focus instead on God's gracious provision for Elijah leading up to that dramatic encounter.

An often overlooked part of this story is that God told the widow to provide for Elijah even before he told Elijah to go and find her. She was obeying God by taking care of Elijah.

Say something like this, **"Boys and girls, today I want to tell you a story about a man named Elijah, who prayed that it would not rain and it didn't! But then he had to trust God to give him food and water! Now before I tell you about how God did that, I have to go and take care of something down the hallway. Will you be good while I'm gone?"** Then step out of the room and return a moment later as the raven! Wear a black sweater or turtleneck. Fly into the room by flapping your arms. Talk in a good raveny voice! Have fun with this. If desired, just use your own words and don't feel too tied to the script.

> **Caw! Caw! My name is Raven, the Raven. Caw! Caw! I was flying along one day when all of a sudden—Caw! Caw! I saw this strange man down by the little river! He looked hungry! Caw! Caw!**
>
> **At first I thought he might want to eat me up! Caw! Caw! Caw! Caw!**
>
> **But then, I saw some of my friends coming and they weren't scared. Caw! Caw! They were bringing him bread—Caw! Caw! And meat! Yummy! Yummy! Caw! Caw!**
>
> **So, I thought God wanted me to help! Caw! Caw! I followed my friends and God led us to a special place where there was bread—Caw! Caw! And meat! Yummy! Yummy! Caw! Caw!**
>
> **But we didn't eat it! We just grabbed some in our beaks—Caw! Caw! Which made it harder to talk, of course. And some in our claws—Claw! Claw!**
>
> **We flew to the hungry man and he was nice to us. He didn't try to eat us, but just took the food and thanked God! Then he thanked us too! Caw! Caw!**
>
> **So every morning and every night we brought him more yummy food in our beaks—**

Caw! Caw! And our claws—Claw! Claw!

Then one day, the river dried up! Caw! Caw! The man was gone, so that day we just ate up all the food ourselves. Yummy! Yummy! Caw! Caw!

I wonder whatever happened to him. He was a nice man and I found out just how much fun it is to serve God—Caw! Caw! With your beak or your claw—Claw! Claw!

Goodbye!

(Fly away, back out the door.)

After you come back into the room, make sure the children know that you are no longer acting like a raven! Then ask them if they were good while you were gone. If they're laughing or accusing you of being the raven, be playful about it, **"What are you talking about? That's silly! Do I look like a giant bird to you?"** Then encourage them to tell you what the big raven talked about. Have them tell you the story the raven told. They'll be reviewing the story as they retell it to you!

(Hint: For today's snack, consider serving bread and meat and water—the same thing Elijah had to eat and drink in the wilderness. A great way to serve both bread and meat would be to make hot dogs! You may even want to gather sticks and have a campfire, to tie in to the second part of today's lesson.)

For the next part of Elijah's adventure, it would probably be fun to make up some simple gestures that the children can do whenever you come to the refrain. If desired, use a big bowl of flour and a couple of cups of cooking oil as props.

Either teach the children the gestures before you begin telling the story, or if you don't think it will be distracting, teach the gestures the first time you come to the refrain.

"Well, kids, I guess I don't have to tell you about how God provided for Elijah during the first part of the drought, but I *can* tell you where he went when the little river dried up: he went to a town called Zarephath!"

After the little river dried up, Elijah went on a walk. God told him to go to the town of Zarephath. "There's a woman there who will take good care of you," said God.

Use the flour, let it pour; *(Sift flour through your fingers.)*
God will give you more and more.
Pour the oil, use it up;
And God will fill your oil cup! *(Pour the cooking oil into another cup.)*

When Elijah came to the edge of town he met a woman who had no husband. She was gathering sticks so she could cook one last meal for her and her son. After that she wouldn't have any food left!

Elijah said, "Trust me! God will keep giving you more food. Now, go and use that wood and food to make us all some supper."

Use the flour, let it pour; *(Sift.)*
God will give you more and more.
Pour the oil, use it up;
And God will fill your oil cup! *(Pour.)*

The woman trusted Elijah. She went home and made supper for him and for her and her son. She had a jar of flour and a small jug of cooking oil. She used it all up to make supper. But later, when she looked into the jar and the jug, they were full again!

Use the flour, let it pour; *(Sift.)*
God will give you more and more.
Pour the oil, use it up;
And God will fill your oil cup! *(Pour.)*

Every day she made more food and every day the flour jar and the oil jug were full again!

Use the flour, let it pour; *(Sift.)*
God will give you more and more.
Pour the oil, use it up;
And God will fill your oil cup! *(Pour.)*

God provided for Elijah and the woman and her son. What do you think—if we trust in God and use what we have to serve him, will he take care of us too? Of course he will!

Use the flour, let it pour; *(Sift.)*
God will give you more and more.
Pour the oil, use it up;
And God will fill your oil cup! *(Pour.)*

If desired, spend some time talking about the important lessons from these stories:

1. Elijah was obedient to God even when it was tough (he had to live out in the wilderness by himself!).

2. God provided for him even when it seemed impossible (first through ravens and then through the widow's cooking).

3. The woman trusted God every day to provide for her, and when she gave her all, without holding anything back, God continued to take care of her.

We can use our gifts to serve God as well. And he will always provide for those who serve him, even in unexpected ways.

Summary

For three long years it didn't rain.
The rain clouds didn't come.
So Elijah needed food to eat
And the ravens brought him some.

Then the river dried up and the food
Was gone and God told Elijah to go
To the town where a woman lived with her son
And God made her flour grow!

God didn't let the food run out
Or the oil in the jar run dry.
So all of them had good food to eat
'Til the rain fell again from the sky.

Chapter 25

Naaman Gets Healed

BASED ON: 2 Kings 5

BIG IDEA: God revealed his love and power by healing a general from one of Israel's neighboring countries.

BACKGROUND: Long ago, leprosy was a dreaded disease for which there was no cure. When a successful general from Aram came down with the disease, all seemed lost until a slave girl mentioned that Elisha could cure him by God's power.

Naaman followed Elisha's instructions and was healed. He became a follower of the Lord and looked for ways to express his thanks to God.

KEY VERSE: "He went down and dipped himself in the Jordan seven times, as the man of God had told him, and his flesh was restored and became clean like that of a young boy" (2 Kings 5:14).

Children might not understand what leprosy is. Explain that the man in the story was sick, or that he had a disease on his skin.

As you tell the story, you (or a storytelling partner) will do actions that correspond to what's happening in the story. The audience then does the same action.

Explain that every time you (or your partner) do an action, the children are going to repeat it. I'd suggest selecting a volunteer to lead the pantomime actions. Give him or her a copy of the script. Have your helper read and practice her part before performing it with you.[6]

WHAT TO SAY:	WHAT TO DO:
Naaman was a soldier in the army.	Salute.
God helped him win many fights!	Put one arm up in victory and stand tall.
He was very strong . . .	Flex your muscles.
and very brave . . .	Make fists and place them on your hips confidently.
And feared no man!	Shake head back and forth.
But he had leprosy, a disease for which there was no cure.	Bite nails on both hands.
Naaman thought he was a goner.	Stick out your tongue and look sick.
He was hopeless.	2 thumbs down.
But wait!	Hold one finger in the air.
A slave girl from Israel had an idea!	Tap your head with your finger.
She'd heard of Elisha, one of God's prophets far away.	Point off into the distance.
And she said, "He'll cure you of leprosy!"	2 thumbs up.
So Naaman asked his boss for sick leave.	Kneel and pretend to plead.
The king told him, "Yes! Hurry and get cured!	Point off into the distance.
Here, take this note and give it to Israel's king."	Pretend to hand the note to someone.
So Naaman left his country with many riches . . .	Rub fingers together like you're holding money.
many camels . . .	Make two humps with your hands.
servants . . .	Bow down with your hands.
and his king's note.	Make a box with your fingers.
After he arrived in Israel he gave the note to Israel's king.	Pretend to hand the note to someone.

The note said, "This is my brave soldier Naaman, please cure him of his leprosy."	Make fists and place them on your hips confidently. 2 thumbs down.
But the king was angry and frightened by the note, so he ripped his clothes.	Pretend to rip your shirt.
He said, "Nobody can cure this guy! He's a goner!	Stick out your tongue and look sick.
I think Naaman's king is trying to start a war with me!"	Shake one finger up and down, scolding style.
Then Elisha the prophet heard that the king had torn his clothes.	Cup a hand behind your ear.
So, he sent a message that he would cure Naaman . . .	2 thumbs up.
And fix the king's problem . . .	Put one fist on top of the other.
(but not the king's clothes.)	Hold shirt and look at "ripped" spot.
So Naaman took his riches . . .	Rub fingers together like you're holding money.
his camels . . .	Make two humps with your hands.
his servants . . .	Bow down with your hands.
and his note.	Make a box with your fingers.
and rode to Elisha's house.	Pretend to ride a horse.
But Elisha stayed inside when Naaman knocked on his door.	Pretend to knock at a door.
He sent his own note to Naaman.	Make a box with your fingers.
"Go wash yourself 7 times in the Jordan River . . .	Pretend to wash armpits.
Your skin will get better . . .	Look over your whole body and smile.
and you will be healed."	Applaud!
(The following section is optional. You may delete it if you wish to shorten the story.)	
But that only made Naaman angry!	Look angry and clench fists.
"I thought he'd come out and call on God's name . . .	Lift up your hands in praise to God.
Wave his hand over the spot . . .	Wave one hand over the other.
and cure me of leprosy!	2 thumbs up.
Our rivers are better than any flowing in Israel!	Make ocean waves with hands.
Who needs this guy or his river?"	Wave hand away and look disgusted.
And Naaman went off in a rage.	Punch one fist into the other.
But Naaman's servants said to him, "Wait, Naaman!	Put one hand up like a stop sign.
Think about this for a minute!	Tap head with one finger
If the prophet had told you to do something great	Hold both hands up in victory.
Wouldn't you have done it?	Hold both hands palm up and look curious.
Why not do this simple thing—wash and be healed!"	Pretend to wash armpits.
(This is the end of the optional section.)	
So Naaman walked down to the river,	Walk in place.
And washed himself 7 times.	Wash armpits.
And his leprosy was gone!	Look over entire body, then put 2 thumbs up.
And Naaman was <u>very</u> happy!	Huge smiles.
Naaman quickly returned to Elisha.	Run in place.
And praised God, for what He'd done.	Put hands up in praise position.
Naaman thanked Elisha	Shake someone's hand vigorously.
and promised to worship the one true God from then on.	Hold both hands up in praise position.
The End.	Bow and have a seat.

Here's a version of the story that uses props. You could either do it in lieu of the storymime on the previous page, or as a review after the storymime.

Long ago there was a man named Naaman. He was a brave soldier, and was very good at using a sword! *(hold up a butter knife)* . . . But one day he discovered that he had a disease called leprosy *(put on a bandage)* . . . If he didn't get healed, he could die!

Then one of the maids remembered Elisha could do miracles by God's power! *(a Bible)*

So, Naaman asked the king if he could go see Elisha, and the king told him to go and take along a note *(a note or notebook)* . . . asking for Elisha's help.

He also took along lots of money *(a handful of coins)* . . . to pay him for his help!

When Naaman arrived, Elisha told him to go and wash seven times in the river *(a bar of soap)* . . . He did as Elisha said and his disease was gone! *(take off the bandage and throw it away)* . . .

He was very happy and promised to worship God from then on *(the Bible)* . . . The end.

Summary

Naaman was a soldier;
Naaman led the men.
But Naaman got sick and thought he'd never lead again.

He heard about a prophet
From a servant girl he knew.
She said, "Elisha can ask God and then he will heal you!"

So Naaman took some camels
And Naaman took some gold
And Naaman went to see Elisha just like he'd been told.

He washed up in the river
Just like the prophet said;
And all the skin that had been sick was smooth and healed instead!

So Naaman was so happy
That he began to run!
He gladly thanked Elisha for all the Lord had done.

Chapter 26

Jonah Runs From God

BASED ON: Jonah 1–4

BIG IDEA: Jonah's prejudice against the people of Nineveh caused him to resent God's compassion toward them.

BACKGROUND: Assyria was an enemy of Israel and was infamous in the ancient world for its cruelty. When God told Jonah to preach repentance to them (Nineveh was their capital city) Jonah ran away. He thought God just might turn their hearts around, and he didn't want the Assyrians to receive God's mercy (see Jonah 4:2).

The book of Jonah ends before we find out if Jonah ever repented of his prejudice.

God's message is for all people and his grace is without bounds. When God wants to show compassion to someone, no matter how bad they might have been, who are we to judge him?

By the way, this is the only book in the Bible that ends with a question!

KEY VERSE: "But Jonah was greatly displeased and became angry. He prayed to the LORD, 'O LORD, is this not what I said when I was still at home? That is why I was so quick to flee to Tarshish. I knew that you are a gracious and compassionate God, slow to anger and abounding in love, a God who relents from sending calamity'" (Jonah 4:1, 2).

The story of Jonah is one of the most popular Bible stories for young children, and also one of the most misunderstood. Many people think that Jonah repented in the belly of the giant fish, but he didn't. He just felt sorry for himself. He never changed his attitude toward the people of Nineveh. And by the end of the story when the people of Nineveh had repented and turned to God, Jonah was still self-centered, just as prejudiced as ever, and pouting like a 5-year-old in the back seat of the minivan!

Since young children might not understand what "prejudice" is, explain that Jonah didn't like the people God had sent him to help, so he ran away.

This book of the Bible isn't about how Jonah repented, but about how God graciously and compassionately showed his mercy—both to the people of Nineveh and to his pouting prophet by giving everyone a second chance.

At the end of the story Jonah's heart was still closed off from loving those people. Sometimes the same thing happens today when a teacher or parent tells two kids to hug each other after fighting! Their bodies go through the actions, but their hearts haven't changed. That's what happened to Jonah. God wants to change our attitudes, lives, and hearts.

Teach the children to cheer or boo for the good and bad parts of this story.

Jonah had a problem. He didn't like the people who lived in a city called Nineveh, and he didn't want them to trust in God! That was bad—BOO!

One day God told him to go and tell the people of Nineveh about him. God loved those people. That was good—YEA!

But Jonah didn't want to do it, so he ran away! That was bad—BOO!

But God still cared about him! That was good—YEA!

God cared so much he sent a storm to get Jonah's attention. But the men on the boat thought they were going to die. That was bad—BOO!

Jonah said, "Throw me in the water and you'll be OK." The sailors did as he said, and the storm stopped! That was good—YEA!

Jonah thought he was going to die. That was bad—BOO!

But he didn't! That was good—YEA!

A fish ate him up! Bad—BOO!

But he was safe in the fish! Good—YEA!

But he still didn't want to obey God! That was bad—BOO!

Then the fish spit him out on a beach. That was good—YEA!

But Jonah still didn't love the people of Nineveh! That was bad—BOO!

But God did! When Jonah finally told them about the Lord they turned to God and God forgave them. And that was very, very good—YEA!

The end.

Children love to hear stories, especially about the embarrassing moments or mistakes of their teachers! This would be a good chance to tell about a time in your life when you ran from God and God came looking for you. What happened? What did God want you to do? What did you do instead? What consequences were there? What did you learn as a result?

When leading the following sound effects story, remember to practice it a couple of times before class to learn the rhythm of the sound effects. Remind the children that you'll be saying each refrain one time through, and then they'll join you and say it two more times.

WHAT TO SAY:	SOUNDS TO MAKE:
Jonah told the people the words of the Lord.	Talk. Talk. Talky talk. Talk. Talk. Talky talk. Talk. Talk. Talky talk.
One day God told him to take a message to some people Jonah didn't like, so Jonah ran away!	Run. Run. Run away. Run. Run. Run away. Run. Run. Run away.
He got onto a boat,	Float. Float. Floaty float. Float. Float. Floaty float. Float. Float. Floaty float.
And sailed away.	Sail. Sail. Saily. Sail. Sail. Sail. Saily. Sail. Sail. Sail. Saily. Sail.
Then Jonah fell asleep.	Snore. Snore. Snory snore. Snore. Snore. Snory snore. Snore. Snore. Snory snore.
Soon, a storm blew in!	Whoosh! Whoosh! Whooshy whoosh! Whoosh! Whoosh! Whooshy whoosh! Whoosh! Whoosh! Whooshy whoosh!
There was thunder!	Boom. Boom. Boomy boom. Boom. Boom. Boomy boom. Boom. Boom. Boomy boom.
And lighting!	Flash. Flash. Flashy flash. Flash. Flash. Flashy flash. Flash. Flash. Flashy flash.
And lots of big waves!	Crash. Crash. Crashy crash! Crash. Crash. Crashy crash! Crash. Crash. Crashy crash!
So the sailors were all very scared!	Shake. Shake. Shaky shake. Shake. Shake. Shaky shake. Shake. Shake. Shaky shake.
They woke Jonah up	Yawn. Yawn. Yawny yawn. Yawn. Yawn. Yawny yawn. Yawn. Yawn. Yawny yawn.

and he told them it was his fault.	Naught. Naught. Naughty naught! Naught. Naught. Naughty naught! Naught. Naught. Naughty naught!
"Throw me overboard," he said. "And the storm will stop." So they did!	Splash! Splash! Splashy splash! Splash! Splash! Splashy splash! Splash! Splash! Splashy splash!
He sank down in the water!	Blub. Blub. Blubby blub. Blub. Blub. Blubby blub. Blub. Blub. Blubby blub.
And a giant fish swallowed him up!	Gulp. Gulp. Gulpy gulp. Gulp. Gulp. Gulpy gulp. Gulp. Gulp. Gulpy gulp.
And he was right! The storm did stop.	Calm. Calm. Calmy calm. Calm. Calm. Calmy calm. Calm. Calm. Calmy calm.
Jonah was sad he was in the fish's tummy.	Waa! Waa! Waa-y Waa! Waa! Waa! Waa-y Waa! Waa! Waa! Waa-y Waa!
Finally, the fish spit him out on the beach.	Burp. Burp. Burpy burp. Burp. Burp. Burpy burp. Burp. Burp. Burpy burp.
Once again God told him to go to the town of Nineveh! This time Jonah went there and told them God's word.	Preach. Preach. Preachy preach. Preach. Preach. Preachy preach. Preach. Preach. Preachy preach.
And even though Jonah still didn't like them,	Pout. Pout. Pouty pout. Pout. Pout. Pouty pout. Pout. Pout. Pouty pout.
The people of Nineveh believed and turned to God!	Hip. Hip. Hip hooray! Hip. Hip. Hip hooray! Hip. Hip. Hip hooray!
The end.	Done. Done. Done-y done. Done. Done. Done-y done. Done. Done. Done-y done.

Summary

Jonah was a prophet.
He was brave and true.
But one day he didn't do
What God wanted him to.

He tried to run away
On a ship to Tarshish.
But the Lord sent a storm
And he sent a giant fish.

The fish swallowed Jonah
And it took him to a beach.
Then he went to the town
And he started to preach.

And even though Jonah
Wasn't very full of love,
The people in the town
Turned to God up above.

Chapter 27

Three Men Stay Alive in the Fiery Furnace

BASED ON: Daniel 3

BIG IDEA: When King Nebuchadnezzar ordered everyone to bow and worship his golden statue, three Jewish men refused to obey. God rescued them and revealed his mighty power to the unbelieving king.

BACKGROUND: King Nebuchadnezzar was one of the most powerful rulers in the world. When he ordered everyone in the land to worship his statue, only a handful of people resisted. When they did, they were thrown into the fiery furnace, but God miraculously rescued them! As a result, the entire empire turned from worshiping the false god to learning about the one true God.

KEY VERSE: "So Shadrach, Meshach and Abednego came out of the fire, and the satraps, prefects, governors and royal advisers crowded around them. They saw that the fire had not harmed their bodies, nor was a hair of their heads singed; their robes were not scorched, and there was no smell of fire on them" (Daniel 3:26, 27).

When you read this story you'll notice the repetition of the list of musical instruments that were played when the people were supposed to bow down to the idol. Also, notice how the rage of the king continues to intensify as the story progresses toward the climax, when his rage turns into amazement and then to awe at the power of Israel's God.

Explain to the children that you're going to tell them a story using a big box of crayons. (You could also use sheets of construction paper, bandanas, or other colorful items. If you have a large class you may wish to use a larger item than a crayon.)

If your children can read, use each crayon to write the appropriate letter. Otherwise, use the crayons to draw pictures that correspond to the parts of the story.

When finished, have the children read the saying (or read it to them). Then, see if they can remember the story and retell it to you based on the different colored letters (or pictures).

FAITH UNDER FIRE

WHAT TO SAY:	SUGGESTED CRAYON:	LETTER TO WRITE:
Once long ago a king put up a tall golden statue.	Gold	O
He told the people to bow down to the ground and worship it!	Brown	U
They were supposed to do that when they heard the musicians play their silver flutes.	Silver	R
But three men wouldn't do it. They only worshiped the God who lives in Heaven and is perfect and holy.	White	(blank)

So, the guards brought the three men to the king. He was rich and was wearing expensive <u>purple clothes</u>.	Purple	G
"I've heard you won't bow down," he said. "This is your last chance! If you don't bow, I'm going to throw you into the <u>fiery furnace</u>!	Orange	O
Now bow when you hear the <u>flutes</u>!"	Silver	D
But they said, "We only worship the God of Heaven! Because only he is <u>perfect and holy</u>!"	White	(blank)
The king was so angry his face was getting <u>red</u>!	Red	C
"That's it!" he yelled. "Make the <u>fire</u> even hotter and throw them in!"	Orange	A
So his guards put more wood on the fire, and <u>smoke</u> went curling up into the sky.	Black	N
But still those three men worshiped the one and only <u>true God</u>.	White	(blank)
Then, guards tied up our three friends with <u>ropes</u>.	Brown	S
And pushed them into the <u>fire</u>!	Orange	A
But they weren't hurt in the fire! They weren't <u>burned up or smoky</u> or anything!	Black	V
The king couldn't believe it! He called for them and they stepped out. The only thing that had burned away were the <u>ropes</u> they'd been tied up with!	Brown	E
"Your God is the greatest!" said the king. "From now on, no one is allowed to say anything bad about their God! He is the only God who is <u>perfect and pure</u> and powerful!"	White	(blank)
And from then on, the men didn't play their <u>silver flutes</u> to worship the idol anymore,	Silver	!
Because they were worshiping <u>the one true God</u>! The end!	White	(blank)

OK kids, we're going to act out parts of this story. I want you to pretend that your body is able to change into anything you want!

First, I want you to pretend that you are that really tall statue! You're 90 feet tall! Ready? 3-2-1 Go! . . . And freeze! Wow! Look how tall all these statues are! I hope none of them tip over in the wind! . . .

Next, let's become like those three brave men who only prayed to the one true God. OK? Ready? 3-2-1 Go! . . . And freeze! . . .

OK! Now, I want you to be that angry king when he found out that the three men were not going to bow down and pray to the statue! He's so mad he can hardly stand it! Ready? 3-2-1 Go! . . . And freeze! . . .

Wow! Now, we're going to become the strong soldiers who tied up the three men. These soldiers are standing right next to the fire, where it was very hot! Ready? 3-2-1 Go! . . . And freeze! . . .

Now, we're going to be the three men and we're inside the fire! But guess what? We're not getting burned up! Instead, we're cool and comfortable and having a good time. Ready? 3-2-1 Go! . . . And freeze! . . .

Wow! You look so comfortable, but guess what? Next we're going to become that king again, but this time he's not angry, he's surprised those men aren't hurt! Let's see how surprised he is! Ready? 3-2-1 Go! . . . And freeze! . . .

Finally, we're going to become the people praising God for saving the three men from the fire. Ready to put your hands up and praise God? 3-2-1 Go! . . . And freeze! . . . Great job, kids!

Summary

The king told the people that they had to obey.
Then he told them to pray to a statue one day.
So most people did what the king had said,
But three men prayed to the Lord instead!

So the king wasn't happy and he yelled at the men.
And he told them, "Don't pray to the Lord again!"
But no matter what he said, those men weren't afraid.
And they just wouldn't bow to the statue he'd made.

So he had the men thrown in a fire nearby,
As the flames leaped up toward the bright blue sky.
But they didn't get hurt and they didn't get burned
And they didn't even seem to be very concerned!

They were safe in the fire that roared and blazed.
And the king was shocked and surprised and amazed!
So he let the men go and he made a decree
That everyone should honor the God of those three.

Chapter 28

Daniel Survives the Lion's Den

BASED ON:	Daniel 6
BIG IDEA:	God rescued Daniel from the lion's den because of Daniel's unshakable faith and his life of integrity.
BACKGROUND:	Daniel had lived in Babylon for decades and had served as an advisor and leader under several different administrations. Through it all, he showed remarkable integrity and conviction. Now, in this story, when his political adversaries try to get rid of him, their plan backfires and they end up eliminating themselves from the equation instead!
KEY VERSE:	"The king was overjoyed and gave orders to lift Daniel out of the den. And when Daniel was lifted from the den, no wound was found on him, because he had trusted in his God" (Daniel 6:23).

Many Old Testament stories have violence in them, as does this popular children's story. You'll probably want to downplay (or avoid bringing up) the fact that the king threw the bad guys into the lion's den where they were ripped limb from limb!

Below is a fun way to encourage children to make sound effects that relate to this story. The children will become louder and softer as you direct them. Say something like this: **"OK kids, I want you to make roaring lion sounds for this story! When I raise my hand, get louder. When I lower my hand, get softer. Let's practice."**

Start with your hand in the middle, raise it slowly higher, and then slowly lower it. Raise it again, then lower it again. Try it a little faster, then slowly again. Be a little silly. Then, put your hand at your side to indicate to the children to be quiet. **"Don't forget that when I put my hand down by my side you'll need to be quiet again!"**

ROAR NO MORE

WHAT TO SAY:	SUGGESTED ACTION:
Daniel stared down into the cave where the lions lived. He could hear them roaring!	Hold your hand in the middle, then raise it up high.
They were really loud.	Raise your hand up higher.
Really, really loud!	Raise it up even higher! *(Drop your hand to your side.)*
The men pushed Daniel into the cave and the lions weren't sure what to do.	Start with your hand in the middle, raise it up and down a bit. Have fun with it! Be a little silly! *(Drop your hand to your side.)*
Then, God's angel shut the mouths of the lions!	Start with your hand in the middle, then lower it really low.
They couldn't roar or bite him or hurt him at all!	Raise it a little, lower it again. Raise a tiny bit, lower it again. *(Drop your hand to your side.)*
Finally, the king pulled Daniel out of the lion's cave and they roared a lot then!	Hold your hand in the middle, then raise it up high.
They were really loud.	Raise your hand up higher.
Really, really loud!	Raise it up even higher! *(Drop your hand to your side.)*

Then, the king pushed the bad guys into the cave and the lions were the loudest of all!	Hold your hand in the middle, then raise it up to the highest position of all.
Daniel was safe because he'd trusted in God! The end!	Bow to the audience.

Here's a chant you can use to review the story!

> **Daniel in the cave,** *(Look around.)*
> **Daniel in the cave,** *(Look.)*
> **Daniel in the lion's cave—ROAR!** *(Look. Roar!)*
> *(Repeat)*
>
> **Prayin' to the Lord,** *(Pretend to pray.)*
> **Prayin' to the Lord,** *(Pray.)*
> **Prayin' to the Lord for help—PLEASE!** *(Pray. Plead!)*
> *(Repeat)*
>
> **Closin' up the mouths,** *(Squeeze the mouths shut.)*
> **Closin' up the mouths,** *(Squeeze.)*
> **Closin' up the lions' mouths—WHEW!** *(Squeeze. Wipe your brow.)*
> *(Repeat)*
>
> **Climbin' on out,** *(Climb out of the cave.)*
> **Climbin' on out,** *(Climb.)*
> **Climbin' on out of the cave—COOL!** *(Climb. Two thumbs up.)*
> *(Repeat)*
>
> **Worshipin' God,** *(Raise your hands high.)*
> **Worshipin' God,** *(Praise.)*
> **Worshipin' God again—YEAH!** *(Praise. Cheer.)*
> *(Repeat)*

One fun and effective way of reviewing stories is to let the children shape their bodies into human statues of the characters or creatures in the story.

When using this technique, it's usually helpful to set a good example for the children by shaping your own body into the appropriate characters. (Note: there's an optional ending that leaves off the part about the bad guys getting eaten up by the lions!)

> **Kids, let's become the different people in this story! Turn your body into those bad guys who wanted Daniel to get eaten by the lions. Ready? 3-2-1 Go! . . . And freeze! Wow! Look at all these bad guys! Yuck!**
>
> **Now, when I count down from three, reshape your body to become like Daniel! Remember he prayed to God. Ready? 3-2-1 Go! . . . And freeze! . . .**
>
> **Now, let's turn into the king! Remember he's sad that Daniel has to go in the lion's cave! I wonder if he'll be sitting on his throne or maybe looking into the lion's cave? 3-2-1 Go! . . . And freeze! . . .**
>
> **Now, we're going to become the lions! Are they mean? Are they hungry? 3-2-1 Go! . . . And freeze! . . .**

Now, let's become God's angel who closed the mouths of the lions! God's angel is big and strong and not afraid of anything! Ready, 3-2-1 Go! . . . And freeze! . . .

Ok, let's become the lions again, but this time, their mouths are shut up tight and they can't bite anyone! Ready, 3-2-1 Go! . . . And freeze! . . .

Wow! And now, we'll be the king again! He's so happy to see Daniel alive! Let's see some happy kings in here. Ready, 3-2-1 Go! . . . And freeze! . . .

(Optional ending.)

Those bad guys who wanted Daniel to get eaten up by the lions got in trouble for being so mean! They got really scared of what the king would do to them. Let's see how scared they were! Ready, 3-2-1 Go! . . . And freeze!

Finally, let's see the lions one last time. They had a good meal by eating up all those bad guys! Let's see a bunch of happy, happy lions! Ready, 3-2-1 Go! . . . And freeze! The end!

Summary

Daniel was a faithful man
Who really liked to pray.
He would worship God or talk to him
At least three times a day.
But some of the other men around
Really wanted him to quit.
Because they didn't like Daniel,
One little bit.

So they complained to the king
And they said it wasn't cool
To pray to God or worship him,
And so they made a rule.
That everyone who prayed to God
Or worshiped him would go
Down in a cave where hungry lions
Waited far below.

So just like always, Daniel prayed,
And so they threw him in.
And the lions thought that
Suppertime was ready to begin.
But God knew Daniel followed him
And always kept his laws.
So he sent an angel to the cave
To shut the lion's jaws.

So in the morning Daniel was safe
And the king was very glad.
And the lions got to eat up all
Those men who acted bad.
And the people in the country
All learned that God can save,
Because he rescued Daniel
From the lions in their cave.

Chapter 29

Esther Bravely Helps the Jews

BASED ON: Esther 1-8

BIG IDEA: Esther's story shows us that God is faithful and works behind the scenes in everyday life to deliver and bless his people.

BACKGROUND: King Xerxes and the Persians had conquered the Babylonians, who had led the Israelites into captivity. In his third year of ruling from the city of Susa, King Xerxes banished his queen. After a nationwide search, he chose a Jewish girl named Esther to be the new queen. This story retells what happened and how God used her courage to protect Jews throughout the empire.

KEY VERSE: "Then Queen Esther answered, 'If I have found favor with you, O king, and if it pleases your majesty, grant me my life—this is my petition. And spare my people—this is my request'" (Esther 7:3).

This is a great story of courage and conviction. Even though God's name doesn't appear in the book of Esther, the lifestyle and faith of true believers rings through every page. (You may need to explain to your students that Jews are people who are all related to a man named Isaac.)

For the following interactive story, if the children can't come up with their own ideas, you can suggest some, but first give them the opportunity to think of fun things to say. It'll give them ownership in the story! (It might be better to make up gestures that you could do for each character rather than refrains for them to say.)

Kids, for this story, you can help me think of fun things to say for the four different people! First of all there's Esther, who is a very pretty girl. What's something a girl might say (or do)? *(Allow them to respond. Affirm them. Choose the funniest or most appropriate response and write it in the space provided below so you don't forget it.)* **OK, next is her relative, a man named Mordecai. He is kind and helpful. What should we say whenever Mordecai talks?** *(Once again, allow them to respond, and write down the choice for Mordecai's line.)*

Next is the king! What's a good saying for him to use? . . . Finally, there's the bad guy, his name is Haman. What should we do or say whenever the bad guy comes into the story? . . . Great! OK kids, I think we're ready to begin!

Esther's part _____
Mordecai's part _____
The king's part _____
Haman's part _____

Long ago there was a pretty Jewish girl named <u>Esther</u> . . . *(insert Esther's saying here).* **She lived with one of her relatives, a man named <u>Mordecai</u> . . .** *(insert Mordecai's saying here).* **He was kind and he worshiped God.**

One day the <u>king</u> . . . *(you get the idea)* **was looking for a woman to be his queen. He chose <u>Esther</u>! . . .**

There was a bad man who worked at the palace who was greedy and thought he was better than everyone else! His name was <u>Haman</u> . . . He wanted everyone to bow down before him, but one man wouldn't do it. That's right, it was <u>Mordecai</u> . . . Since he wouldn't bow to him, <u>Haman</u> . . . wanted to get rid of him and all the other Jews. He didn't know Queen <u>Esther</u> . . . was a Jew!

Well, word spread throughout the land of his evil plan. And soon all the Jews heard about it, including <u>Mordecai</u> . . . He told <u>Esther</u> . . . and asked her to see if her husband, the <u>king</u> . . . could help save the Jews.

So, she told the <u>king</u> . . . someone was trying to get rid of her and all her people. "Who would do such a thing?!" he asked.

"It's him," she cried. "It's <u>Haman</u>! . . . "

Well, when her husband heard that, he told the guards to take that bad man away and then, he gave his job to the kind and faithful <u>Mordecai</u> . . .

By being brave and trusting that she was doing the right thing, the queen had helped to save her people. And I doubt you'll ever forget her name. It was <u>Esther</u>! . . .

The end!

Notice that an unsung hero in this story is Mordecai. He stood up for what he believed in, refused to compromise his convictions, and challenged Esther to boldly use her position of influence to help her people. (See Esther 4:13, 14.) Some of us need to have the courage of Esther, and some of us need to have the resolve of Mordecai. Both of them remain as powerful examples of boldness, bravery, and conviction.

Let's act out part of the story!

Queen Esther, the king, and Haman were at a party. They were dancing . . . and eating . . . and finally, Esther told everyone to be quiet. Shh . . . Then she started crying! . . .

The king was surprised! . . . He asked her what was wrong. And Esther pointed at Haman . . . and said, "He wants to kill me!" Let's say that just like Esther did. Ready: "HE WANTS TO KILL ME!"

The king was so mad . . . madder than that . . . even madder! . . . He told the guards to take that bad man away, and they did. Let's wave goodbye to Haman! . . .

Then he kissed Queen Esther! Everyone make kissy lips! . . .

And everyone, except Haman, all lived happily ever after.

The end!

Summary

Esther was pretty and Esther was brave.
And Esther knew how she was s'posed to behave.
When the king was unhappy and feeling alone,
He chose her to be the new queen on the throne!

But a bad man named Haman had made a mean plan
To kill all the Jews who lived in the land.
So when Esther found out, she talked to the king
And he asked her, "Who would do such a terrible thing?"

She answered, "It's Haman, he's evil you see.
He wants to kill all of my family and me!"
So the king stopped the plan and sent Haman away.
And so all of the Jews were rescued that day!

Yes, Esther was pretty and Esther was brave
And Esther knew how she was s'posed to behave.
She helped save her people. She did what she could.
Oh, Esther was beautiful, brave, and good.

Chapter 30

Nehemiah Rebuilds the Walls

BASED ON: Nehemiah

BIG IDEA: Nehemiah was a man of both action and prayer. He worked hard while still trusting in God to make his prayers come true.

BACKGROUND: When Jerusalem was overrun by the Babylonians, the Jewish leaders and ruling class were deported. Later, the Persians took over. After 70 years in exile, Prince Zerubbabel and a priest named Ezra returned to Jerusalem to rebuild the city.

However, after nearly 15 years, the walls remained in ruins. Hanani, one of the new inhabitants in Jerusalem, traveled the 1000 miles to visit his brother, Nehemiah, in the court of the King of Persia. He told Nehemiah about the condition of the city.

After bringing up the matter to God in prayer, Nehemiah set off to oversee the rebuilding of the city himself. Nehemiah was a detailed planner, a shrewd politician, a brave leader, and a humble man of prayer.

KEY VERSE: "So the wall was completed on the twenty-fifth of Elul, in fifty-two days. When all our enemies heard about this, all the surrounding nations were afraid and lost their self-confidence, because they realized that this work had been done with the help of our God" (Nehemiah 6:15, 16).

Be ready to explain some of the cultural details of this story that might not be familiar to children today. For example, *city walls* were built to protect people from others who might want to harm them. Nehemiah worked as the *cupbearer* for the king. That was an important job that meant he had to make sure the food was safe for the king. The king trusted him and they were friends.

Since this story might not be too familiar to your students, it would probably be a good idea to tell the story first in a simple way, before adding too many creative drama or interactive storytelling ideas.

> **Kids, long ago, some of God's people lived in the city of Jerusalem. They thought they were safe from their enemies because they had big walls all around their city. But one day, their enemies knocked down the walls and made the people move far away! They were sad and missed their homes in Jerusalem.**
>
> **Finally, some of them went back to live there, but still the walls were all knocked down.**
>
> **Now, one of God's men was named Nehemiah. He worked for the king far away. When he heard that the walls were still knocked down, he knew his friends and family weren't safe! He cried and was very sad. But he prayed and then asked the king if he could go and help the people rebuild the walls. The king was his friend and said he could go.**
>
> **So, Nehemiah went back to Jerusalem. He planned how to build the walls. He was a good leader. The people listened to him and obeyed him. Even though bad guys tried to stop him and hurt him, Nehemiah prayed a lot and God protected them.**
>
> **Soon, the walls were built and everyone in the city was happy. They thanked God and had a big party. The bad guys had lost and God's people were safe in the city again!**
>
> **The end.**

As you go through each verse of the following story song, act it out! The children will enjoy the repetition and the opportunity for creative movement.

(Refrain—clap on the beat)
They built the walls,
They built the walls,
They built the city walls!

Sometimes they were hammering! (hammer)
Sometimes they were carrying! (carry)
Sometimes they were piling up the heavy, heavy rocks! (pile up the rocks)

(Refrain)

Sometimes they were sleeping . . . (sleep)
Sometimes they were creeping . . . (tiptoe)
Sometimes they were lifting bricks up high above their heads! (lift the bricks)

(Refrain)

Bad guys tried to stop them. (pound your fist in your hand)
Bad guys tried to hurt them. (shake your fist in the air)
Bad guys tried to make them quit and move far away. (point off into the distance)

(Refrain)

Nehemiah prayed to God. (fold hands in prayer)
Nehemiah trusted God. (nod and smile)
Nehemiah knew that God would help them with their work. (tap your head)

(Refrain)

God heard all the praying men. (fold hands in prayer)
God saw all the working men. (hammer)
God helped and protected them and they finished up the walls! (raise hands in praise)

(Refrain)

When leading the following activity, you may wish to change the amount of time you give the students to build their wall based on the size of your class. Also, be sure to be very encouraging during the first couple of attempts so they don't get frustrated.

Play the game as long as you like, or until each child has had the chance to be either Nehemiah or The Bad Guy.

Let's play a game to review today's story! So, I'm going to yell out the name of someone in the room and they'll be The Bad Guy. Then I'm going to yell out someone else's name and that person is going to be Nehemiah. Everyone else has only 5 seconds to grab hands and form a wall between Nehemiah and The Bad Guy to protect Nehemiah from the men who want to hurt him!

Ready to build a big wall around Nehemiah? Let's practice! I'll be The Bad Guy and (insert the name of one of your students) **is going to be Nehemiah! Go! 5-4-3-2-1!**

Summary

The city was in ruins
The walls had fallen down.
Enemies could get the people
Living in the town!

Nehemiah heard the news
And Nehemiah prayed.
He went to help the people
Who were lonely and afraid.

He told the people where to work
And taught them what to do.
He trusted God would help them all,
Until the work was through.

And soon the walls were built up tall
And all the work was done.
The Lord had helped them do their work
And guarded everyone!

Understanding Young Children

Young children present special challenges for the creative storyteller. After all, their little bodies aren't made for sitting still! They wiggle and squirm and run around and look at birds flying past the window and play with their shoelaces and just want to have fun!

In this chapter, you'll learn five characteristics of young minds, and how each characteristic affects how you can more effectively communicate with children.[7]

Abstract vs. Concrete

Young children don't think in abstract terms. They won't easily understand the hidden meanings, metaphors, and symbolism in stories. Usually, the power of parables comes from weaving a spiritual truth into a story that's essentially about something else. The more abstract the parallels, the less young children will grasp their meaning.

For example, when Jesus told a story about a lost sheep, he was using a story about an event from his culture to show the similarities of how we spiritually wander from God, and how God takes the initiative to look for us and rescue us—and then celebrates when we're found.

But for young children, it's a story about a lost sheep. Period. They won't understand all the spiritual parallels.

This doesn't mean you should *never* tell parables to young children, just be aware that you may need to explain the symbolism in as concrete a way as you can: "That shepherd cared for the sheep enough to go and find it and bring it home. God loves us just like that. He loves you and wants to bring you home to heaven."

So, as you craft stories for young children, look for simple, clear, easy-to-understand stories that are concrete rather than abstract.

Sitting Still vs. Paying Attention

One day when my daughter Ariel was four years old I dropped her off at a church's day care program. When I picked her up a few hours later and asked her if she had fun, she shook her head no.

"Why not?" I asked.

"We watched a movie."

"Well that sounds like fun. Why wasn't it fun?"

Then she explained that the teacher had told them that if they moved during the movie, they wouldn't get a snack.

"Well, what was the movie about?" I asked.

"I don't know," Ariel replied. She'd been concentrating so hard on not moving, that she couldn't pay attention to the movie!

Don't mistake sitting still for paying attention. Listening is not the same thing as sitting still. For many young children, sitting motionless is much more work than paying attention. And it's nearly impossible for them to do both at the same time.

Listening, really listening, is tiring. It's not the same as watching TV, because when you listen to a story, you're responsible for creating all of the images of the story in your mind. Remember, children love listening to stories, but sitting still while someone talks to them sounds like a lot of work and not a whole lot of fun. So, focus more time and energy on grabbing and keeping the attention of the children rather than trying to get them to sit still.

Some people claim that young children have a short attention span. "Children can only pay attention for one minute for each year they are old," someone told me once. I struggled with that because, while I understood where this woman was coming from, I'd seen preschool children sit and listen to me telling stories for twenty-five minutes or more at a time.

Then one day, early childhood expert and author Mary Manz Simon asked me, "Do you think children have a short attention span?"

As I fumbled for an answer she said, "If they did, Steven, how could they play in the bathtub for half an hour at a time?"

Yes! I'd finally found someone who shared my perspective!

I think the secret is that children don't have a short attention span; they have a large distraction span! If they're interested, engaged, and involved they'll be able to pay close attention for quite a while. But they can also be easily distracted. So be sure to remove distractions before starting your story. Make sure there isn't a door behind you that someone might walk through, or other teachers preparing snacks in view of the children, or music from another room floating through the walls.

The challenge is to tell stories in a way that your students can understand and relate to, that engages their imaginations, and that actively involves their bodies.

How do we do this? By choosing appropriate material, taking the time to prepare and shape it so that it connects with our students, and then by telling our stories with energy, imagination, enthusiasm, and participation.

One more thing: sometimes it's helpful to give children a mental break in-between stories. Chant a Bible verse with them, do an object lesson, have a short contest, or do a brief skit. Then, after you've given their imaginations a quick break, transition into the next story.

Reading vs. Telling

One night, I finished reading a bedtime story to my oldest daughter (who was two years old at the time) and closed the book.

She snuggled close to me and said, "Daddy, can you tell me a story with your mouth?"

"What do you mean, Honey?" I asked. "I just read you a story!"

And then it hit me.

"Do you want me to tell you a story without the book?"

Her eyes lit up. "Uh-huh!"

I learned an important lesson that day: she didn't want a story from the pages of a book, but from the pages of my heart. She wanted me to tell it with my mouth.

Many educators simply read each lesson or story from their church's Bible curriculum. While there's nothing wrong with studying the ideas found in your curriculum, be aware that the way the story is written in this book (or any other) is not necessarily the "right" way for you to tell it to your students. You're a different storyteller than the author, and your class is unique. It's much more important for you to connect the story to the lives of your students than to "get through the material" in each lesson.

So look for ways to learn and tell the story yourself (from your own mouth and in your own way!) rather than just reading it from the pages of a book.

Explaining Stories vs. Telling Stories

For the most part, children (and adults) will pay attention only as long as they're curious about what's happening. In other words, if you're telling a story and the children know how it will end or how it will get to the end, they begin to lose interest. Children will start thinking about snack time, crafts, or playing on the playground.

So, use your children's natural curiosity to your advantage. Don't tell them what the story will be about. Instead, do all you can to ignite and foster their curiosity!

I've found that the more time I spend preparing my lessons, the less time I end up lecturing, and the more the children end up learning. But the less time I spend preparing my lessons, the more I lecture and the less they learn.

If kids aren't having fun, they probably aren't learning. And if kids are interested and engaged in the lesson, they probably aren't misbehaving.

So spend more time preparing your lessons and thinking through transitions from one activity to another. Look for ways to include more learning activities, attention-getting object lessons, and interactive storytelling in your teaching time.

If things get boring, direct the attention of the students to another activity. Remove distractions and keep the children focused. A good rule of thumb to remember is this: the younger the children you're speaking to, the shorter you'll want to make the stories you're telling. Also, the more you explain a story, the less impact it has. So spend less time and effort explaining what every story is supposed to mean and more effort telling it in an exciting and engaging way in the first place.

Asking Questions vs. Telling Stories

Have you ever heard (or said!) something like this?

"OK, boys and girls, today we're going to learn about Noah and the ark! Noah took lots of animals on the ark. What were some of the animals? That's right, he took horses. Horses live on farms. Has anyone ever been to a farm? What did you see? Were there cows there? Cows give us milk to drink in our cereal. What's your favorite type of cereal? . . ."

I can just picture what happens when the parents pick up their children, "So, Joey, what did you learn at Sunday School today?"

"I don't know. . . . Something about how Noah fed Fruit Loops to the horses on the ark. . . ."

Asking children too many questions while you tell a story can bewilder children, distract them, and lead you into tangents. So, ask fewer questions and don't be afraid to just tell the story.

Sometimes teachers ask all these questions "to get them to pay attention." But a poorly directed question will often distract rather than focus children.

Many educators, when telling the story of "Jonah and The Big Fish," say things like, "Boys and girls, today's story is about a great big fish. Ooh! Who likes to go fishing? Wow!"

Now, the problem with this approach is that, without realizing it, you've just changed the subject. Instead of thinking about Jonah, the children are thinking about a fishing adventure they've been on. And then, a few minutes later when the children want to talk about their fishing trip, the teacher feels like they "aren't paying attention to the story." In truth, they were paying attention, but then got sidetracked by the teacher's question! And besides, Jonah has nothing to do with a fishing trip. No one goes fishing in the story so why bring up a fishing trip in the first place?

Whenever you ask questions, make sure they're not open-ended questions that will get the children thinking about something other than the story you're telling.

If you ask any questions, let each question direct attention to the main point of the story: "Kids, how many of you have ever been afraid of getting in trouble?" (As you ask this, raise your own hand so they know to answer with their hands, not their mouths.) "How many of you have ever said 'No!' when your mommy or daddy asked you to do something? Me, too! Today's story is about a man who lived long ago who said 'No!' to God . . ."

Remember, every question you ask must move the story forward, not cause your children to become distracted from the story.

So, in summary,

• Young children can't sit still for long. They love to move, play and wiggle—it's how they pay attention! So find ways to help them wiggle during the stories and be patient with them if they move around a little during the storytelling time.

• Young children love to play pretend. So, foster and nurture their curiosity, imagination, and sense of wonder.

• Young children would rather hear a story told than explained. So, tell your stories in an exciting way and make your summaries and sermons short, concrete, and to the point.

• Young children can't understand abstract concepts. So, avoid elaborate analogies and metaphors and focus instead on simple stories and illustrations from your children's world.

• Young children are easily distracted. So make sure you've created a storytelling environment that has few (or no!) distracting things to look at, listen to, touch, or do.

20 Ways to Let Young Children Know You Love Them[8]

• **Notice me.** It's easy to look over my head, ignore me, or step around me. Take the time to get down on my level and look me in the eyes. I never want to feel like I'm in the way.

• **When I put my arms up toward you, hug me.** Sometimes I just need to be held, even if it's only for a moment.

• **Tell me the truth, but not all of it at once.** I'm not ready to hear some things yet. Just a little bit at a time. Be patient. And don't worry; I'll believe you even if I don't understand you.

• **Snuggle with me on rainy days.**

• **Be gentle with words.** Sticks and stones may break my bones, but words may bruise my heart.

• **Protect me from the dark places, the bullies, and the monsters of the world.** I can be easily frightened, intimidated, and misled. Sometimes I need you to guard me and stand up for me.

• **Smile at me.** It makes me feel welcomed, loved, and important!

• **Share my excitement when something special happens.** I love to celebrate life! Join me!

• **Forgive me quickly.** I promise I'll do the same for you. And tell me that God isn't angry at me anymore, either.

• **Go ahead and tickle me, but stop when I ask you to.**

• **Let me giggle and fall over laughing sometimes.** And join me when I do! Remember, it's OK to be silly. It doesn't mean you're childish, just childlike.

• **Teach me when it's OK to cry.** Be willing to dry my tears when they come. Comfort me when I'm scared and let me know that I'll be safe whenever I'm with you.

• **Admit your mistakes.** Remember, I'm watching you to learn how a big person should act.

• **Pray with me.** Pray for me. And teach me to pray, too.

• **Spend time with me, even if it's not doing anything special.** I want you to be my friend and I just like being with people who care about me. I'll bet you do, too!

• **Let me wish. And dream. And pretend.** These are great ways to help me to learn that the most important things in life are all invisible.

• **Discipline me when I misbehave.** Sometimes I'll disobey just to see if you notice. Even though I don't like to be punished, I'm glad you care enough to teach me right from wrong.

• **Remember that hugs speak louder than words.**

• **Listen to me, especially when I'm sad.** That's when I really need a friend.

• **Tell me every day how much God loves me.** And show me what that kind of love looks like in the real world.

How to Make Your Stories SOAR!

Now that we've explored some of the characteristics of this age group, let's look at some specific ways you can creatively and effectively tell stories to young children.

Step 1
Study the story

When a pilot taxis down the runway, he knows where he's going to land before he takes off. He begins with his destination in mind. Storytellers do the same thing! We begin with the end in mind. We start by looking at the end of the story first.

The beginning of a story is more than just the first thing that happens in a story. The beginning is the originating action, the one that sets in motion all that will follow. And the end of the story is the resolution. So look closely at the story as a whole. To grasp what a story is really about, ask what's going on, who struggles, what they discover, and how that changes their life or situation.

Sometimes as you study a story, you'll realize that some of the language or content of the story isn't appropriate for young children. Take King David, for example. His adventures were often bloody, brutal, and very graphic. His sins (murder, adultery, and pride) resulted in the deaths of tens of thousands of people! Yet, David is a favorite for curriculum authors of stories for young children. While he's certainly a great hero of the faith, you need to be careful when telling his stories so that you don't frighten, shock, or confuse young children.

Step 2
Look for ways to include participation

I like to keep the acronym SOAR in mind when I'm preparing stories for children ages 3-7. It was the starting point of every chapter in this book and, when you understand the concepts involved, you'll be able to come up with engaging, fun, and interesting ways of telling stories to young children all by yourself.

Sounds OAR

The first thing to look for in a story is **sounds**. What sounds naturally occur in this story? Could the children make sound effects? Maybe animals appear in the story and you can make the animal sounds, or maybe the children can recreate the sound of the storm that Jesus calmed, or the snoring disciples in the Garden of Gethsemane. Search for sounds that you and the children can make to keep everyone engaged in the story.

Here are seven ways to incorporate music, instruments, sound effects, chants, rhythm, and rhymes in your storytelling.

> **1. Make music with instruments:** Use simple instruments such as kazoos, bells, xylophones, rain sticks, wood blocks, drums, maracas, or tambourines to allow children to make music during some (or all) of the story. You can use the instrument yourself, have a small group of children accompany you, or you can give instruments to the whole class!
>
> You may wish to create your own simple rhythm instruments with beans, sticks, cardboard tubes, sand, or shells. Pour beans or sand into a container, seal the opening, and you've got a shaker! You can also use instruments to create background sounds or music for specific sections of your story.
>
> **2. Make music with your body:** Children can join you by clapping their hands, tapping their feet, snapping their fingers, slapping their knees, or rubbing their hands together! (The younger the children, the tougher it'll be for them to "keep a beat." So be patient!)

3. Make music by singing: Songs often appear in Bible stories. Many times when David was going through a tough time, he wrote a song about it! As you tell those stories, you could sing lines from the Psalms he wrote.

Or make up simple melodies for the refrains of your stories, sing worship songs, or listen to songs that summarize Bible stories. You may wish to sing a popular song or hymn and then tell the story about the person who wrote it, or when and why it was written.

4. Make music with a cheer, chant, or rap: Think of a cheer, chant, or rap that you can use as a refrain for the story. Create a way of telling the whole story, or part of the story, in rhyme!

If you have a large group, you may wish to divide the audience into sections or groups and assign each section a different part or refrain to say or sing.

5. Make music by adding a call and response section: When using "call and response" storytelling, you read or say a section of the story and the audience responds by saying or doing something.

Some Psalms are set up this way. See Psalm 136 for an example of a simple story-song that includes a refrain your children could say or sing!

6. Add mood music: Find instrumental music that reflects the mood of the story. Or, look for CDs with sound effects that a helper can cue during the telling of the story, or search online and download appropriate sound effects. You may even have a talented instrumentalist at your church who can improvise music on a keyboard or guitar as you tell the story!

7. Make your own sound effects: A story rich in sounds is the story of Noah's Ark (Genesis 6-9). You could reenact the sounds of the building process (cutting wood, stacking, painting), the sounds of the animals (roaring, chirping, howling), the sounds of evil people (grunting, screaming, cackling) and the sounds of the storm (raining, blowing, thundering).

Sound effects are easy to add whenever there are animals, specific environments in your stories (such as jungles, night scenes, or crowded markets), or weather-related scenes (such as storms, wind, or thunder). Cue the audience when to participate, when to get louder, and when to be as soft as possible. You can also invite the children to join you by booing or cheering during different sections of a story!

Sounds Objects **AR**

Next, look for **objects** that appear in the story, or brainstorm ways that you could use simple objects to help you tell the story.

For example, you may wish to use a surprise bag when you tell stories. As you tell the story, pull out objects for the students to see, smell, touch, or taste. They'll pay close attention because they'll wonder what you're going to pull out next!

Here are nine ideas for using simple costumes, props, and objects for telling stories to young children.

1. Wear a silly costume: Keep the costume simple—perhaps just a hat, sunglasses, or a wig. Children love it when adults wear silly clothes or goofy costumes. Having a few simple costume pieces on hand can add lots of fun to the stories you tell.

2. Use a puppet: Consider using finger puppets, hand puppets, or arm puppets. Remember when using a puppet to (1) only open and close its mouth on each syllable (i.e. as you open and close your own mouth), (2) always keep the puppet moving, and (3) have the puppet look at whomever he is talking to. By following these three simple steps, you'll create the illusion that the puppet is alive and it won't matter that you move your lips when you tell the story.

3. Bring out the toys: Use stuffed animals, toys, dolls, army men, and action figures as props.

4. Serve food: Eat foods that are referred to in the story, eaten in the story, or related to the story. Create your own edible object lessons using pretzels, gum drops, marshmallows, raisins, crackers, cheese, apple slices, or peanut butter (warning: some children are seriously allergic to peanuts!).

5. Tell a story with a felt board: Use cut-out felt figures and a colorful background to tell the story. There are many fine felt boards and figures commercially available.

6. Hand out scarves: Use crepe paper, ribbons, streamers, banners, or scarves to represent fire, wind or water. Have children wave them at appropriate times in the story.

7. Blow bubbles: Blow bubbles whenever God or an angel speaks in a story.

8. Sensory Props: By appealing to the senses you'll help the children better remember the stories.
- **Sight**—Turn off the lights, flicker them, or use filters to create different-colored lighting.
- **Touch**—Use squirt guns when telling stories of storms, rain, or floods. Use fingerpaints with younger children. Use a fan to create wind, or a hair dryer to create a hot desert wind!
- **Hearing**—Add music, sound effects, or funny noises to the story.
- **Taste**—Eat food that relates to the story. Something sweet (like honey) can represent manna or God's Word!
- **Smell**—Place candy or oranges in a bag to create a sweet smell. Use stinky garbage to represent sin!

9. Manipulatives: Use anything that can be changed into another shape or form to show the transition of the main character, or to represent different objects that appear throughout the story.
- paper can be cut, crinkled, or folded.
- aluminum foil can be squeezed, flattened, or molded.
- pipe cleaners can be bent, twisted, or curled.
- string can be cut, tied, or designed.

Sounds Objects Actions R

Third, look for **actions** that appear in the story, or for ways to act out what happens in the story. You can use creative dramatics to help introduce the story you wish to tell, dramatize the story as you tell it, or review the story after you've finished telling it.

Whenever you invite the students to join you in movement or creative dramatics, be sure to create an atmosphere in which participation is safe, encouraged, and fun. Invite people to participate but don't force them to. Clearly explain when you want the children to join you, what you want them to do, and when they should stop. You might say, "Whenever I put on my hat you'll start making the sound of the lions in the cave, but when I take it off, you'll stop. Let's practice . . ."

Remember, you can have students use their fingers, gestures, facial expressions, or they can use their whole bodies to act out parts of the story. Consider using sign language, bouncing in place, pretending to walk, waving arms, tapping feet, or using other simple movements. (Be aware that younger children may have a tough time clapping and singing at the same time.) Exaggerated actions are funniest, so let loose and have fun!

Sounds Objects Actions Repetition

Finally, look for **repetition** that naturally occurs within the story. It might be the repetition of a specific phrase (such as, "And God looked at what he'd made and it was good!") or a series of events. For example, when God was calling to Samuel in 1 Samuel 3, repetition occurs as God calls to Samuel, Samuel runs to see what Eli wants (since he thinks the voice is Eli), and Eli sends him back to bed. This process happens three times. You could create a refrain to say each time Samuel runs to Eli, or have the children run back and forth from different sides of the room whenever you come to that part of the story.

Repetition occurs naturally in many types of stories. For example, think of the stories of "The Three Bears," "The Three Little Pigs," or "The Three Billy Goats Gruff." See how the number "3" occurs in each of them? Now, think of Scripture. How many times did Peter deny Jesus? Three. How many times did Jesus ask Peter if he loved him? Three. How many people came up to the Good Samaritan as he lay in the ditch? Three. How many times did Jesus return to the sleeping disciples in the Garden of Gethsemane? Three! See all that repetition?

God knows we remember things best when they're repeated. That's how we're wired to remember them. And that's why God imbedded repetition all throughout his story in the Bible!

Every time you find repetition, you can invite the children to say or act out a part of the story with you.

Step 3
Put it all together

Many people think they're not very creative, but usually they can come up with great ideas if only they would begin by limiting themselves in specific ways. For example, limiting yourself to thinking of specific sounds, objects, actions, or repetitious sections that appear in the story. Once we do that, we discover that we're a lot more creative than we ever thought we were.

I was teaching a creative storytelling seminar in Ohio one time when a first grade teacher came up to me and said, "I wish I were creative like you. I'm just not creative. I can't think of anything to do with my students. Can you come teach my class?"

"Well, what lesson are you teaching?"

She sighed. "The story of Jesus calming the storm. But I'm just not creative like you."

"Well," I said, "first you need to limit yourself. Think of ways to help the story SOAR. Are there any sounds in the story?"

She nodded. "Yes, there's the sound of the storm and the sleeping disciples. We could make the sound of thunder or rain falling on the water or the snoring disciples, but I'm just not creative. I wish I was creative like you."

"Um, are there any objects in the story?"

She took a deep breath. "Well, there's water and a boat and Jesus is laying his head on a pillow. So, we could maybe get a blue blanket and all hold the edges and put something in the middle of it, like a ball or something, and that could be the boat and we could all shake the blanket to make the storm and then hold it still when the water is calmed, but I just can't think of anything."

"OK, what about actions?" I asked, looking at her curiously. "Are there any actions in the story?"

She sighed again. "I suppose we could act out being the raindrops or we could swing our arms to make the waves or we could pretend to be sleeping and then get up as Jesus did. Half the class could be the storm and the other half the disciples. Oh, can't you come teach my class, you're so creative!"

By then I was getting a bit exasperated. She was so full of ideas but she just couldn't see it because she'd been telling herself for so many years how uncreative she was! "What about repetition?" I asked.

"Yes, yes, there's repetition. The rain falling and the disciples trying to wake Jesus and the waves rushing against the boat. I guess we could make up a refrain or something, I just wish I were creative like you."

"I wish I were creative like you!" I said. And only then did it begin to dawn on her that she could come up with creative ideas all on her own.

Once you begin to think in terms of sounds, objects, actions, and repetition, you won't even need a book like this! You'll have more ideas than you could ever need. (But this will be our little secret. Don't tell your friends this until after they've bought a copy for themselves.)

Practice your story, but don't try to memorize it. Feel free to change the story and adapt it (even while you're telling it)! And trust that God will use you to impact young lives when you're faithful in serving him.

Oh, one more thing. You won't always use all of these ideas (sounds, objects, actions, and repetition) for every story. That would be a bit too much. Instead, use each idea judiciously.

Also, remember to let the way you tell the story grow out of your own personality, gifts, and interests. It's more important for you to connect with the students than for you to read the story as it's found in this (or any) book. Feel free to change the story to make better use of your own special God-given gifts and to more appropriately connect with your students. To review, here are the steps to follow when developing the stories you are going to tell:

1. Read the story in context and try to discover what's going on in the background. Look for the big picture. Study the context. Who were the listeners? Why was this story told? Often the context of the story will give you clues about the point of the story or the intended application of the story.

2. Figure out what the story is really about. Don't worry so much about being able to summarize the story in a tidy little topical sentence. Instead, try to let the story move you to the place where God wants you to be. Connect with the story not just in your head, but also in your heart.

Then, look for a natural way to let the audience reach that point too (without your having to explain to them what they're supposed to be feeling). As you retell the story, ask, "Who changes? How is she at the beginning of the story? How is she different at the end of the story?"

3. Look at the structure of the story. Some stories have lots of action; others have lots of dialogue. Ask yourself, "Is this a story that I mainly *hear*, or one that I mainly *see*? How might that affect the way I retell it to my students?"

Some stories have lots of repetition. What about this story? If not, what's the flow of the action? Where does the action occur? Does the setting or scenery change throughout the story? How will the different scenes help you remember the flow of the story?

4. Think about how you're going to retell this story. Are there issues or events that occur in this story that might be inappropriate for the age group you're teaching? How will you handle those?

As you think about how to tell the story, always keep your students in mind. How will your children respond to this story? Are there concepts or words that your students won't understand? If so, what are some similar words you could use that'll help the children better relate to the story?

5. Practice telling yourself about the story. Try to picture it for yourself. Try retelling the story in your own words and describe what you see. How will you describe the scenery or the characters in a way that will help your listeners picture them in their own imaginations? What images, characters, or events in this story move you? How can you weave those emotions into the story?

6. Connect creative storytelling techniques to the story. Look for ways to include sounds, objects, actions, and repetition in retelling the story. Think of ways to make the story memorable, engaging, and interactive. Ask yourself if there are specific storytelling techniques that naturally lend themselves to this story (for example, audience participation, music, silly props, creative dramatics, etc.). Then, weave those into the way that you practice and rehearse the story.

7. Prepare your story with your audience in mind. You've taken the time to better understand your story, to think through the flow of the story, to personally connect with it, and you've looked for creative ways to retell it. Now it's time to practice your story with your students in mind. Pay special attention to the beginning, the ending, and the transitions to and from any audience participation sections.

Avoid the temptation to "polish" the story in a specific way; rather, spend your time really getting to know the story so that you can adapt it to your specific audience and respond to the reaction of the children as you tell the story. As you practice the story, pay attention to how it's going and keep any changes, phrases, or comments that add to the story. Have fun, relax, enjoy yourself, and trust that God will do something exciting as you let yourself be used by him.

Ten Tips for Telling Stories to Young Children

1. Speak With Respect—A strange thing happens to many otherwise normal adults when they start to tell stories to young children. They begin talking in a sappy, sing-songy voice that doesn't sound real or genuine. It makes me think of Barney on helium! Don't talk down to your students. Instead, talk to them in a natural, energetic, and lively way that doesn't belittle them.

2. Choose Appropriate Stories—Some stories in Scripture deal with themes and issues that young children aren't ready to understand or even hear about. Not all parents agree on which subjects their children should be exposed to at a young age. So be honest but not always forthcoming about what information appears in the stories you're teaching young children. Avoid dealing with death, sex, violence, adult themes and adult language in your stories. Leave out graphic details that young kids aren't ready to hear.

3. Start at the End—Before beginning to work on your story, read through the story in the Bible. Look at what comes before and after the story to see the context in which it was told. Take the time to really study and get to the heart of the story. Then, look for the main point of the story and see who it's really about. Avoid stories with too many characters or too much symbolism. Ask yourself, "Will my students really understand this story?" Especially with younger children, ask what changes in wording, content, or order you may need to make to the story.

4. Create Simple Refrains—Look for repetition, simple plots, and simple resolutions. Nail down the main idea and then add a chant, movement, or instrument.

5. Stay Focused on the Story—Rather than asking lots of questions during the story (which can distract the children), stay focused on the action and emotion of the story. As you tell the story, watch your students. Look at their faces to see if they understand and enjoy the story. You can usually tell if you're making a story too long or too frightening by the size of your students' eyes. Keep the stories short, simple, and action-packed.

6. Look for Connections—As you study and prepare your story, look for sounds, objects, actions, and repetition in the story. If you can find ways to connect the story to music, creative dramatics, or movement, you'll be able to easily include audience involvement.

7. Tell the Story Your Own Way—Tell the story in your own words; don't try to remember "the right words." Use natural gestures. Some people "talk with their hands." If that's natural for you, great! If not, don't try to imitate someone else. Do what's most natural for you. Funny faces, funny voices, and silly costumes will work well for this age group!

8. Move Through the Story—Let your body help you tell the story. If a character in your story is large and scary, stand big and lower your voice. If the character is tiny, scrunch up small. As you practice the story, practice your movement, inflection, and gestures.

9. Tell the Story First—This book includes hundreds of helpful ideas and storytelling suggestions for audience participation. However, if your children are unfamiliar with a story, you might wish to tell the story first and then invite them to act out the story so that the children understand what's going on in the story and can remember the sequence of events. Then, after telling the whole story, say, *"OK, everyone! Now, let's have some fun with this story! Let's act it out"*

10. Relax and Enjoy! —Smile and have fun as you tell your stories. Value this time of connection with your students. Tell the story with lots of expression and don't be afraid to get a little silly. Rely on God and let him work through you!

1 (page 6) Ok, so some Bible scholars believe that it didn't rain until the flood, but I think it's still OK if you let the kids act like rain here on day 2!

2 (page 8) This poem first appeared in *Believe It: Bible Basics that Won't Break Your Brain* (Standard, 2003) by Steven James. Used by permission.

3 (page 11) This poem first appeared in *Believe It: Bible Basics that Won't Break Your Brain* (Standard, 2003) by Steven James. Used by permission.

4 (page 30) An earlier version of this storymime first appeared in my book *24 Tandem Bible Stories* (Standard Publishing). Used by permission.

5 (page 37) This poem first appeared in *Believe It: Bible Basics that Won't Break Your Brain* (Standard, 2003) by Steven James. Used by permission.

6 (page 80) An earlier version of this storymime first appeared in *The Creative Storytelling Guide for Children's Ministry* (Standard, 2002) by Steven James. Used by permission.

7 (page 97) Some of the content in the appendices is based on material from *The Creative Storytelling Guide for Children's Ministry* (Standard, 2002), and *Sharable Parables* (Standard, 2005) by Steven James. Used by permission. The information has been adapted and expanded for this book.

8 (page 101) Excerpted from *"Fill 'Em Up"* a Children's Ministry Seminar written by Steven James for the International Network of Children's Ministry. © 2001. All rights reserved. Used by permission.

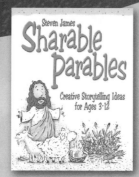
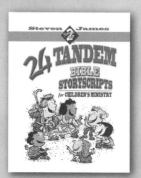